How to Make Your Long-Distance Relationship Work and Flourish

A Couple's Guide to Being Apart and Staying Happy

Tamsen Butler

HOW TO MAKE YOUR LONG-DISTANCE RELATIONSHIP WORK AND FLOURISH: A COUPLE'S GUIDE TO BEING APART AND STAYING HAPPY

Library of Congress Cataloging-in-Publication Data

Butler, Tamsen, 1974-
  How to make your long-distance relationship work and flourish : a couple's guide to being apart and staying happy / by Tamsen Butler.
     p. cm.
  Includes bibliographical references and index.
  ISBN 978-1-60138-578-9 (alk. paper) -- ISBN 1-60138-578-1 (alk. paper) 1. Spouses. 2. Interpersonal relations. 3. Interpersonal communication. I. Title.
  HQ734.B943 2012
  302--dc23
                              2012001641

Printed in the United States

INTERIOR LAYOUT: Antoinette D'Amore • addesign@videotron.ca
COVER DESIGNS: Jackie Miller • millerjackiej@gmail.com

Printed on Recycled Paper

A few years back we lost our beloved pet dog Bear, who was not only our best and dearest friend but also the "Vice President of Sunshine" here at Atlantic Publishing. He did not receive a salary but worked tirelessly 24 hours a day to please his parents.

Bear was a rescue dog who turned around and showered myself, my wife, Sherri, his grandparents Jean, Bob, and Nancy, and every person and animal he met (well, maybe not rabbits) with friendship and love. He made a lot of people smile every day.

We wanted you to know a portion of the profits of this book will be donated in Bear's memory to local animal shelters, parks, conservation organizations, and other individuals and nonprofit organizations in need of assistance.

– *Douglas & Sherri Brown*

PS: We have since adopted two more rescue dogs: first Scout, and the following year, Ginger. They were both mixed golden retrievers who needed a home.

Want to help animals and the world? Here are a dozen easy suggestions you and your family can implement today:

- *Adopt and rescue a pet from a local shelter.*
- *Support local and no-kill animal shelters.*
- *Plant a tree to honor someone you love.*
- *Be a developer — put up some birdhouses.*
- *Buy live, potted Christmas trees and replant them.*
- *Make sure you spend time with your animals each day.*
- *Save natural resources by recycling and buying recycled products.*
- *Drink tap water, or filter your own water at home.*
- *Whenever possible, limit your use of or do not use pesticides.*
- *If you eat seafood, make sustainable choices.*
- *Support your local farmers market.*
- *Get outside. Visit a park, volunteer, walk your dog, or ride your bike.*

Five years ago, Atlantic Publishing signed the Green Press Initiative. These guidelines promote environmentally friendly practices, such as using recycled stock and vegetable-based inks, avoiding waste, choosing energy-efficient resources, and promoting a no-pulping policy. We now use 100-percent recycled stock on all our books. The results: in one year, switching to post-consumer recycled stock saved 24 mature trees, 5,000 gallons of water, the equivalent of the total energy used for one home in a year, and the equivalent of the greenhouse gases from one car driven for a year.

Disclaimer

The material in this book is provided for informational purposes and as a general guide to the challenges and rewards of participating in a long-distance relationship. This book should not be a substitute for professional psychological or relationship counseling.

Acknowledgments

For Rae Crusoe, who is the calmest military spouse I have ever met, and Stacy Grajkowski, who is always willing to lend a listening ear when my long-distance arrangement gets to be overwhelming.

Also, for my husband Scott, who was in Afghanistan the entire time it took me to write this book. I am proud of your military service, but I look forward to the day when I can stop being a first-hand expert on long-distance relationships.

Table of Contents

Chapter 2: The Nitty-Gritty: Money, Children, and House Rules   43

Chapter 3: Communication is the Key   67

Chapter 4: The Masks People Wear   117

Chapter 5: Setting Goals   133

Chapter 6:
Flourish Solo and Together   153

Chapter 7: The Long-Distance Date   175

Chapter 8: Visiting Time   191

Chapter 9:
Avoid BeingYour Own Worst Enemy   211

Chapter 10:
Knowing When to Call It Quits   239

Introduction

t is not difficult to spot a happy couple. The way they look at each other, the way they reach for each other's hands when walking down the street, and the way they seem oblivious to the world around them are all clues that these two people unequivocally belong to each other.

What happens when there is no looking into each other's eyes, and there are no hands to hold when walking down the street? Is it possible to maintain a solid relationship when two people are separated by miles, time zones, and in some cases, an almost complete lack of communication for long periods? Can love flourish from afar?

The answer is a resounding "yes." Being in a long-distance relationship does not doom you and your partner to eventually losing your feelings for each other. Like any other successful relationship, these long-distance romances need to be given attention and cultivated to flourish. Although it is true that long-distance relationships can take quite a bit of effort, most relationships take effort. No relationship is without its difficulties, and just because miles separate you does not mean you cannot make it work.

These Relationships Can Work

Some people find that the time they spend away from their partners serves to strengthen their relationship. Think of relationships where two partners have never been apart. Do they know if they can trust each other when separated by miles? Do they know that absence makes the heart grow fonder? Do they know if they are strong as individuals and as a couple? People in successful long-distance relationships can boast these claims because they know them to be true from their own experiences.

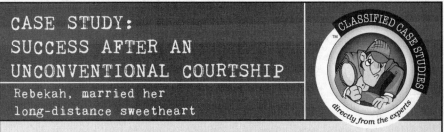

CASE STUDY: SUCCESS AFTER AN UNCONVENTIONAL COURTSHIP

Rebekah, married her long-distance sweetheart

I guess you could call it love at first sight when I first talked to Darren on voice chat while gaming online. He was from England and his accent was so appealing and sexy to me that I was fascinated with him. He was funny and charming along with being sweet and witty. We became quick friends. A few weeks went on, and we were connecting on a more personal and social level. It alarmed me a bit considering I was not interested in a relationship at the moment, much less interested in a one that was an ocean away.

Things progressed, and during winter vacation, we spent every waking moment together from afar. With the six-hour time difference, I thought it would have been extremely difficult to keep in touch, but Darren was devoted to "us." I would come home from work and talk to him until he passed out from exhaustion. Some days, it was seven or eight hours spent talking and playing online, and on weekends, we spent up to 15 hours. It was a new experience for me. I had dated men before that who were right in front of me, yet who would not devote their time to me as he had. In such a short time, I was falling in love with this man.

I decided at our anniversary of six months of courtship that we should meet on a common ground, so we met in Florida. I wanted so desperately to feel his arms around me. We spent a week of bliss together. He met my family, and we spent the week in Disney World®, feeling like teenagers. I got to know his pet peeves and the little annoying things he does, and he got to know mine. It was during that trip that he kneeled down and proposed.

It takes a lot of paperwork and red tape to get married in the United States to someone who is not a citizen, so we were not able to get married quite as quickly as I would have liked. We had to make an effort to stay connected during this time while we waited for clearance for him to fly back over for our wedding. I know if it was not for our devotion to the relationship, and the constant care we put in to it, we would not be married today. Long-distance relationships are not meant for the weary or the easily distracted. It is extremely difficult and emotional, but if you truly love someone, you can endure it. If both parties are honest and willing to share in each other's lives, it will be a beautiful thing. You become best friends, but it will not work if only one person is putting forth the effort. You both have to compromise and learn about each other, just like any other relationship.

When love endures physical time apart, it is a love that has been tested and has come out victorious on the other end. Not all couples can say their relationships have been tested and have overcome the odds.

These Relationships Take Work

No claim will be made in the pages of this book that long-distance relationships are easy; it is tough being away from someone you love, and it can be difficult to dedicate yourself to someone whom you do not see on a regular basis. Whether you find yourself sitting alone at a dinner party because your significant other is not around, or you get misty-eyed because you spy a couple snuggling on a park bench, there are everyday reminders that you are in a situation that is not the norm.

Consider an example of a traditional couple that sits together in a room reading from separate books. They are not necessarily interacting, but they are still together and are sharing an experience. Now, consider a couple in separate cities that is sitting in their own respective spaces and reading from books. These two couples are engaged in the same act of relaxing and reading, but the couple in the same room derives the additional benefit of being physically close. The moment strengthens the traditional couple, but for the long-distance couple, it is simply another afternoon spent reading.

Long-distance relationships are not passive arrangements. For many people, however, love — or the possibility of love — is worth the extra effort. There are ways to transform everyday moments like sitting and reading into a moment that helps strengthen your relationship, whether it is by sharing the moment using technology or learning how to use solitary moments to recharge your own batteries, so you have more strength to deal with having a loved one away.

My Story

Tamsen Butler and her husband, Scott.
Courtesy of Tamsen Butler

I am certainly not a stranger to long-distance relationships. One of my first serious relationships was with a man who lived in North Carolina while I lived in California. Although we remain friends today, that relationship is a case study in how to fail dismally in a long-distance relationship. We did not communicate with each other and never set any boundaries regarding our behavior while away from each other. In hindsight, I can see how that relationship was doomed to fail. In present day, my husband's military career has made him cumulatively absent for about three of the past eight years. Sometimes, he is in another state, and sometimes, he is on the other side of the globe. He had to learn how to deal with leaving his wife and kids behind, while I had to learn how to deal with being left behind. Our relationship would not have endured had we not been willing to figure out this whole long-distance thing.

I do not make the claim to handle his physical absence gracefully each time. At times, I have to fight the feeling of having been abandoned, and there are times when I get upset because no one is at home to vent my frustrations to at the end of a challenging day. It sometimes seems unfair that I committed to a man who is frequently absent.

For me, it has been a constant learning process. I had to figure out the best ways to communicate my feelings to my husband without overburdening him. I had to figure out how to enjoy my time alone, which is not a simple task for an extrovert like me who craves socialization incessantly. It has been an important evolution in our relationship, one that is obvious to me when I compare the first time he went away when we were newlyweds (I cried, pouted, and imagined him gallivanting around town with other women.) to the most recent time he had to pack up and leave (I asked him for a power of attorney and double-checked to make sure Skype™ worked on my laptop.). Preparing for his absence has become second nature, and, I dare say, there can be distinct advantages to long-distance relationships, even if you do not have a choice in the matter.

Tamsen's Tip

I joke with my friends that my favorite thing about my husband being gone is a tie between having the entire bed to myself at night and having control over the television remote after the kids have gone to sleep for the night.

I will point out these advantages and give extra tips in the "Tamsen's Tip" sidebars throughout the book. The information in these sidebars is coming from my own personal experiences with long-distance relationships. I have been there, and I continue to be there. Allow me to help ease some of the pain that can come with having a loved one far away and deal with and redirect your frustrations so you can thrive solo and together. You are not alone.

This Book Will Help You Make It Work

This book presents advice from a variety of sources. You will read stories from people from different walks of life who have managed to make long-distance relationships work and from people who can look back and figure out why these relationships did not work for them. Expert advice also is provided throughout, so you will get the benefit of words of wisdom from couples that have been there and hear from relationship professionals who study the topic of long-distance relationships on an academic level.

This helpful guide will help you keep your relationship active, even from a distance. You also will find tips and reminders about keeping everything else going while your partner is away, whether that means managing a household budget or getting out for time with your friends. The importance of communication is stressed, and you will find ways to ensure that you present your true self to your partner, even if it is over the phone, over the computer, or in person.

Use this book to help you and your partner set goals for your relationship and to spot when trouble is brewing (and how to stop trouble before it becomes big trouble). It will help you make your relationship thrive splendidly, even if you cannot spend time lovingly glancing into each other's eyes or walking down the street hand in hand.

Chapter 1

Love Takes All Kinds

Not everyone who lands in a long-distance relationship does so intentionally. Although some couples make the conscious decision to maintain a relationship despite the miles, plenty of couples start out in traditional relationships and have to adjust to a long-distance arrangement because of circumstances beyond their control. No matter what the reason for the arrangement, being successful in a long-distance relationship takes extra effort.

Although there are not many formal studies regarding the number of couples currently involved in long-distance relationships, most estimates place the number of people in long-distance relationships to somewhere around 9 or 10 million. It is difficult to assess the number of people involved in long-distance relationships for several reasons. Relationships come and go, so this is not a constant number. Also, people who are in committed long-distance relationships may not have the opportunity to report their status for official purposes such as the Census.

An informal study by the website **www.longdistancerelation ships.com** revealed some interesting statistics about people in long-distance relationships. Of the respondents (who were all involved in long-distance relationships when participating), the average distance between the partners was 125 miles. Long-distance couples visited each other one or two times a month, and when they called each other on the phone, they typically spent 30 minutes talking. The average duration of the long-distance arrangement among respondents was 14 months.

Your relationship might not fit within these statistics, and there is nothing wrong with that. Once you learn what works best for you and your partner, you will have your guidelines on how your relationship best runs. Whether your methods correspond with what the majority of other couples in long-distance relationships are doing is not relevant; what matters is what allows your relationship to flourish.

Tamsen's Tip

Long-distance relationships are sometimes referred to as "LDRs," especially online.

It Is Worth the Effort?

Nearly anyone who has been in a long-distance relationship knows how tough it can be to maintain a relationship, let alone feel connected despite the miles. Yet, plenty of couples start out — or wind up — in a long-distance relationship and manage to flourish. Being in a long-distance relationship has its unique issues, many of which quickly can evolve into full-blown problems. On the other hand, if you are in a long-distance relationship already, then you also realize that there is a reason you allow yourself to remain in this relationship despite the challenges. Whether you are convinced that you are with your soul mate, or you are so deeply invested in the relationship that ending things because of the distance is not an option, consider this time away from your partner to be a unique opportunity to prove the resilience of your mutual commitment.

People from successful relationships commonly can reference a time in their relationship when they were tested. When a relationship can overcome the odds — such as when the relationship can withstand a long-distance arrangement — it serves as a potent reminder to the couple that they can get through things together. A unified front resulting from a couple conquering an obstacle can be a powerful thing.

Tamsen's Tip

When you feel alone, physical distance does not change the love you and your partner feel for each other. Remind yourself that someone out there loves you and is willing to be with you despite the miles. When you think of things in those terms, it makes your relationship seem more incredible.

Make no mistake about it: Being in a long-distance relationship can be tough. Sometimes you just want someone to hug you and tell you everything is going to be fine after a long, hard day. It can be hard to come home to an empty house after a frustrating day at work or stay home day in and day out with small children while a spouse is away. When it comes right down to it, however, if there is real potential for the relationship to be forever — or if you already know it is destined to be forever — then a long-distance arrangement is just another facet of your relationship to deal with.

CASE STUDY: MAKING IT WORK

Ashlee, not worried about the distance

I met Cody on prom night.

After the prom, I went to a friend's house, and across the street just so happened to be Cody's house. I had never met him before, but my friend swore that Cody and I would be perfect together. When I did not show the interest she was looking for in meeting Cody, she refused to get out of my car and demanded that I march over to Cody's house to meet him. So, there I went, in my prom dress, to meet Cody for the first time.

He was so sweet. We all hung out and after awhile, he offered to get me something comfortable to wear. He let me borrow a sweater and pajama pants, so I did not have to sit around in my prom dress. We hit it off right away, and I did not think twice about starting a relationship with him, even though we lived two hours away from each other. I already drove to his area about once a month to visit my friend, so as far as I was concerned, it was not unreasonable to think we could make it work.

The most difficult thing about being in a long-distance relationship was the time in between our visits, although the times when I had to leave to drive back home were a close second. I often wound up calling into work because I could not manage to leave Cody. On the bright side, I did get to concentrate on my schoolwork more when I was home because I was not with Cody. I also got to enjoy the time I had with him more than I might have if we lived close to each other. When we were together, it felt like a mini-vacation of happiness.

If I were to give advice to other people who are thinking about getting into a long-distance relationship, it would be this: Do what you want. If it is worth it to you, then it is worth doing. Cody and I are getting married in June of 2012; being his girlfriend while living two hours away was worth it for me.

How Did You Land Here?

Some couples have never known anything but a long-distance relationship, while others land in a long-distance relationship despite their best attempts to stay close to each other geographically. The difficulty of a long-distance relationship also can vary depending on the people involved. Although some couples can thrive while maintaining completely different households miles apart, some couples experience drastic strain from recurring weekends apart. All long-distance relationships take work, but some scenarios can be tougher than others.

Separated by circumstances

Not everyone sets out to have a long-distance relationship. Sometimes circumstances occur that lead to a decision needing to be made: stay together long-distance or end the relationship? If you are among those who chose to stay together despite the miles, you might have landed there because you or your partner headed off to college or received a job offer elsewhere. When you cannot make the choice to follow your partner for whatever reason, you might land unexpectedly in a long-distance relationship. The dynamics of the relationship can change drastically, and if both partners cannot adjust to the new arrangement, it can cause serious problems or prove to be the end of the relationship.

Extra tension in a relationship can occur when both partners do not necessarily agree about the arrangement. Suppose a boyfriend accepts a job promotion that forces him to move to another state, and this is after the girlfriend implored him not to accept the promotion because she could not move, and she feared the distance would ruin the relationship. This relationship has to deal with the miles separating them and the underlying resentment both people might experience (him for feeling she did not support him, and her feeling he did not care enough to stay). Unless concerns are expressed and talked through, this couple will have the odds stacked against them. *You will learn more about the importance of communication — and how to leave the lines of communication wide open — in Chapter 3.*

Even when both people agree to maintain a long-distance relationship, and even when they are in total agreement about the circumstances leading up to the arrangement, extra tension can abound. Sometimes, it is just difficult to be alone, even in a relationship. One of the expectations for relationships includes companionship, and when your relationship does not provide companionship in the traditional way (hugging, smiles, etc.), it can make it a difficult arrangement.

CASE STUDY: EXPERT ADVICE

Tina B. Tessina, Ph.D.
AKA "Dr. Romance"
Licensed psychotherapist and author
of Money, Sex and Kids: Stop Fighting
about the Three Things That Can Ruin
Your Marriage

Long-term commutes offer benefits and problems. The benefits are that you have time to establish a routine, support systems, and even develop a re-entry system that works. The problems are that you are spending time apart, and keeping your connection and intimacy feeling fresh is not easy. When you are separated, or the time you have together is scarce for a long time, you need to change your routines for keeping in contact and maintaining a strong emotional connection.

You might be surprised to find that the people you spent time with as a couple are not as comfortable when you are a single, and the activities you are used to might not work as well. If this turns out to be your situation, you will need to plan to find different social networks and activities. If your partner is away for an extended time, he or she also might need to find a social network. Changing the people you spend time with and your activities can present awkward transitions and concerns from your partner.

If you are apart for a long time, you might need to find a different way to make decisions long distance about bill paying, hiring help, and budgeting. Especially if the away partner is sometimes incommunicado, the stay-at-home partner needs to have the ability and permission to make unilateral decisions and to know what the parameters are. This can create an uncomfortable change in the power structure of your partnership.

Commuting for an extended period can be lonely for both partners, and even if you have close family relationships or strong friendships while apart, it does not replace "pillow talk," physical affection, and shared experience. The changes you will make to do that are another transition that could be awkward and uncomfortable at first. Making your commuter relationship work begins with getting as realistic a picture of your situation as you can, making plans to solve each problem that you envision, and learning to solve new issues that arise on the spot.

Separated perpetually

It is common for two people to fall in love despite geographic distance. Whether the couple meets online, meets while one of them is just visiting, or another circumstance, sometimes an attraction is too strong to ignore despite the distance. Couples who have an exclusive relationship, but who have never experienced anything but a long-distance relationship together, are at an advantage and a disadvantage. On the one hand, they do not know anything but the distance, so they cannot complain about how things once were because long distance has always been the norm for them. On the other hand, some might argue that it is nearly impossible to get to know someone well enough if they have never spent more than a few days in close proximity to each other (or have never laid eyes on each other, which is often the case with relationships that begin online).

Tamsen's Tip

If this is not your first long-distance relationship, acknowledge that every relationship is unique. Just because your previous relationship did not work, it does not mean that this relationship is doomed to fail, too.

These relationships have unique issues. How can you know that the image your partner presents to you is who he or she is, considering you have never had the opportunity to be with each other throughout a variety of situations? When you do not get the opportunity to witness how your partner reacts in times of stress, when upset, or when emotionally distraught, it can be difficult to get the big picture of whom that person is. Couples in this situation who flourish are those couples who communicate well and who do not put on masks to portray someone they are not. *You will learn more about the masks people wear in long-distance relationships in Chapter 4.*

CASE STUDY: MAKING IT WORK

Sara, college student

I suppose we were just at a point where it did not make sense to stay in the same city anymore — financially, career goals, etc. I feel lucky to be with someone committed enough to me and willing to be flexible. Breaking up was never discussed. We had been together for around a year when I graduated college, and he quit a job he did not like at all. At this point, we did not have any real direction for our relationship carved in stone. So, we decided that it was going to make the most sense long term to do things long-distance for a bit. We each moved back home with our parents. The way I picture it in my head sometimes — and what helps me deal with how much I miss him and all the other issues a long-distance relationship can bring — is sort of like a picture of the structure of DNA: together, split, together again. In this modern world, I imagine there are couples who have more (DNA transcription) bubbles than others, but perhaps shorter stretches (of nucleic acids) in between. If it is not yet obvious, I am a microbiology fan, so I cannot help but look at things in this way.

In our relationship, that is just it. We struggle with figuring out where and when the bubble will close up, and we will be able to be together again. Physically, that is. For us, there is not exactly a clear finish line in sight. At the same time, we are committed to making things work. So, for the past few months we have each made efforts to visit one another and stay connected every day. We have traveled and met in Washington, D.C., and he has visited me in my hometown of Omaha. I plan to visit him soon in California.

There is one big challenge: it is expensive. That is part of why we typically stay at our parents' houses or where we can secure free room and board. There are also issues of time — finding the time to talk on the phone when it is convenient in each of our schedules and with the time-zone difference. The problem of sheer absence makes keeping the fire hot (if you will) a little difficult, and we have to find creative ways to stay connected. We also have to relate to what each other and what we are doing independently. For lack of a more articulate way to put it, there are also times where I am tired, insecure, and sad, and it just sucks being apart.

We talk on the phone at least once a day. We also email and text things to each other at least once a day. We Skype when we can. Lately, we have been trying to make the same recipe for dinner once a week and video chat while we do so. Occasionally, we will send things to each other via snail mail: photos, postcards, and gifts. In general, I think we are pretty good communicators. We are honest and let each other know when something is bothering us. That is a good idea, long-distance or not.

I keep myself busy. Without us being in the same place, I do not feel pressure to cut back on certain commitments to make time for a dinner date, etc. At the same time, I realize I probably would not allow myself to be so busy if we were physically together and would make the time to spend with him instead of being so busy with my own things. Staying busy is absolutely a coping mechanism for me, as well as a way to save money to travel to visit him and open up options for us down the road. Other advantages — if you want to look at them this way — are that when we do finally get a chance to be together, it is more deliberate than ever, which is romantic. It forces us to plan to do things we may not have ever done otherwise if we were caught up in daily routines together and to attempt to not sweat the small stuff. If we have only a certain number of days together, we are not going to spend that time arguing. Even if we do disagree, we are more apt to resolve things and move on more quickly.

Stressful distance

Long-distance relationships can be stressful, but what happens when one of the partners is in a dangerous situation? When a partner leaves for a military deployment or is incarcerated, the stress levels of both partners can be elevated exponentially. It can be difficult enough to be separated by miles and time zones, but when one partner has limited capabilities to communicate or is in potential danger (or both), extra stress is added to an already stressful situation.

The stress of danger and limited communication affect more than just the person in danger. The partner left at home might deal with intense fear that something is going to happen to the other person, and this fear can have a significant impact on the relationship and on every facet of that person's life. When a person spends most of the day worrying that something terrible is going to happen to the other person, it can be hard to thrive, let alone function.

It is possible to flourish in a long-distance relationship even when one member of the couple is stuck in a potentially dangerous environment. *You will learn about dealing with this special long-distance arrangement in Chapter 9.*

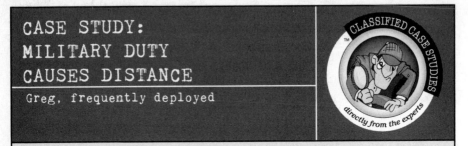

CASE STUDY:
MILITARY DUTY
CAUSES DISTANCE

Greg, frequently deployed

We spend time preparing before I leave. Logistically, Patti runs the household finances to make deployments easier, and that enables a smooth transition from that point. The first thing I do is get powers of attorney for the cars, child care, military ID cards, the house, or anything else that might pop up, and I get Patti a set of the military orders because she might need those. I fix what I can find wrong with the house and cars; this is always a sore spot because everything seems to break the day after I leave.

Emotionally, we spend as much family time together as possible. The last time I deployed, we had my mom fly out to help take care of my son while Patti was in her last semester of school. We break the news to our son slowly in the span of a few months so that he is prepared for the separation. If we wait too long to tell him, he is an emotional wreck. It seems to me that Patti handles the separation for the first month or two but then gets overwhelmed with the separation and having to do everything at home by herself.

I think it is harder to prepare emotionally for the time apart because we have done this enough times, so logistically, it is just second nature. However, preparing emotionally does not get any easier. Sure, you know what to expect and how to deal with it, but you know that you are going to miss your family. You know they are going to have a hard time without you and that they will miss you. Trying to balance time with your wife, children, and friends can be daunting.

When I am away, Patti and I Skype nightly. That is the biggest form of communication we have. Keeping in touch gives a sense of being with your family. Last year while I was in Korea, I even spent three hours at my son's birthday party over Skype. Care packages are the next best thing. Getting things that you cannot get away from home — especially homemade baked goods — are a hit and even cheer up people you are not related to if you share. Mail is nice, also, but it is not as important to me as it is to my 8-year-old son Jimmy.

Patti tries to keep me at ease while I am away. Just letting me know she is there for me is huge. I like when she tells me how her day went. It is petty on my behalf, but sometimes I get uncomfortable when she goes out with her friends, so talking to her before and after her night out puts me at ease. I believe she feels the same way when I get an opportunity for a night out with the guys when I am deployed.

The hardest thing about being away is missing special days, such as anniversaries, birthdays, Christmas, and my son's first day at karate. My year in Korea was the hardest for Patti as well; she had to trust that I would behave myself, and in a place like Korea, it is easy to do something stupid. When I am deployed to Iraq or Afghanistan, she knows I can be in harm's way, but I think it is easier to compartmentalize that than whether I will go out to drink and get into trouble.

If I had to think of an advantage to our time apart, I would say that it strengthens our relationship. When I return from a deployment, I feel a new sense of respect for what Patti accomplishes. The advantages do not outweigh the cons, though.

Support and Reactions

The type of long-distance relationship you have will affect the reaction you get from other people when talking about your partner. For example, although military spouses can expect to receive offers of help and sentiments of gratitude for their partner's service, people who choose a long-distance arrangement for other reasons, such as one partner moving to another state to pursue a higher paying position while the other partner stays so the children can finish the school year, might have to deal with people saying unintentionally hurtful things, such as, "Do you think it is best for your children to be away from one of their parents?"

Couples who maintain long-distance relationships because their romance started online might feel the need to defend their relationship; even though more couples are meeting online, there can still be a stigma attached to online romances, which makes people apprehensive to talk openly about the difficulty of being apart.

The key is to have people you can talk to openly about the difficulties in maintaining a long-distance relationship, whether it is close friends, a support group, a licensed therapist, or someone else who is willing to help you deal with any relationship frustrations. This might take the form of a casual conversation over coffee riddled with venting frustrations or something more formal, where you talk with someone trained to assist people in your situation. Either way, seeking out support — regardless of the reasons for landing in a long-distance relationship — will be helpful if you seek help from the right people. *Chapters 5 and 6 will help you decide whom to turn to for help and who might not necessarily be looking out for your best interests.*

Tamsen's Tip

There is no shame in turning to a therapist for help. Visiting a therapist does not mean there is something fundamentally wrong with you but instead just means you need a neutral person to listen to your feelings and ideas. Seek out a therapist who is well versed in helping people with long-distance relationships, and you will have a strong ally.

Banish negative talk

Guard your pessimistic thoughts and words that come out of your mouth. Suppose you try to call your partner, you receive his or her voice mail, and the intrusive and unfounded thought that he or she might be with another man or woman pops into your mind. If you have no basis for this thought beyond receiving his or her voice mail, learn to banish this type of thought. On a similar note, do not accept these similar ideas from the people around you.

Why is it important not to allow your imagination to get the best of you when you are in a long-distance relationship? Long-distance relationships can work, but they take work. If you are in a long-distance relationship with someone whom you have committed to, or whom you think might be "The One," do not let miles be the end of your relationship. Instead, replace negative thoughts with positive ones, accept that your relationship will not be perfect, and move forward with your partner despite the physical distance. There is a chance the effort will be worth it in the end.

Chapter 2

The Nitty-Gritty: Money, Children, and House Rules

This chapter is not going to be romantic, but it is full of important information that can help your long-distance relationship flourish. Any time two people try to maintain a relationship from afar, there are bound to be logistical things that need to be dealt with, and problems could arise if these details are ignored. One person might assume that the other person is dealing with something one way, only for it to turn out that the other person is dealing with it a different way or not dealing with it. An unpaid mortgage or a furnace that breaks after going without maintenance checks can add strain to a relationship that is already experiencing stress from the distance.

So, although composing a household budget or mapping out the household rules might not seem like a romantic task, it will help your relationship flourish nonetheless. When the nitty-gritty details are taken care of, you and your partner can spend more energy making each other feel secure and loved in the relationship. Figure out the particulars about how finances should be handled, how children should be disciplined, and the other important details, so you have the energy to cultivate your relationship.

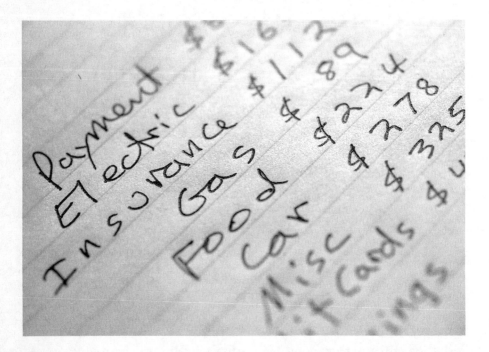

If you are currently in a long-distance relationship where you do not share households, finances, children, or anything else you might need to be on the same page about, you still might want to have a conversation about these details to make sure you are both in agreement. You might find you want to take your long-distance relationship to the next level, and if you have already covered the basics, then it will be easier to take that step.

CASE STUDY:
TAKE CARE OF YOURSELF
AND THINK PRACTICALLY

Detra, running the household

Give yourself love. It is all right if your emotions are unpredictable and your life is chaotic while running a household without your partner there. Just do what works best for you, and try not to worry about the rest. It is a cliché, but literally take one day and one problem at a time. You cannot plan everything and control every situation, so try to be flexible. Things can be unpredictable from beginning to end. Some things are easier. For instance, housekeeping is easy because I have extra time without my hubby. I also have someone come clean the house once a week. This is a huge help, practically and emotionally. If you have children, make sure you both get social time.

We recorded my husband reading books for the children to watch before bed whenever they choose. We use Skype when it is possible. My husband and I read the same spiritual books, so we continue to grow together and feel connected. The right books help us find the silver lining during the stressful times.

You have to be selfish when you are running a household with a spouse who is not there. I get manicures and pedicures, which I used to think were selfish, but now I see them as relaxing ways to spend the extra time I have. My evenings are for me to recharge and relax. I read books I have been waiting to read and watch entire television series I had never had time for before.

Preparing to Talk

Some relationships enjoy communication that allows conversations about household basics to occur organically. If you are in a relationship in which one or both of you enjoy composing a budget or discussing discipline tactics for the children, then these conversations might seem like second nature to you. If this is the case, then keeping the lines of communication open and working together might be all you need to make sure everything is taken care of. On the other hand, if you are like most couples, you will have to make a concerted effort to set time aside to discuss the nitty-gritty details.

Start by setting time aside with your partner to discuss basic things, and make sure your partner knows you want to do this in an attempt to make sure things run smoothly. Make it a collaborative effort if possible; if your partner works 80 hours a week or is deployed across the globe for a military operation, you might not have the luxury of spending hours figuring out a household budget. Be realistic in your expectations of what your partner can contribute to this discussion, but be clear in your intentions. For example, do not barrage your partner with budget questions over the phone before first making it clear you intend to have a discussion about finances so you can work collaboratively to manage household finances.

Time your discussion well. If you have to have this talk over the phone or computer, set a specific time to make sure you agree that the conversation will center on whatever topic you have to tackle. The problem with not making it clear beforehand that the discussion will center around relationship business is that your partner might come away from the conversation feeling unfulfilled emotionally. Think how you would feel if you called your partner to connect emotionally and wound up talking about the checkbook. Set a date and time to have this discussion because this will prepare both of you to get to business and could prove to strengthen your relationship. After all, successfully tackling a problem together can make your relationship feel more solid.

You might not have the luxury of preplanning when these discussions will take place. If your partner can contact you only sporadically, or if an emergency comes up, you will have to have the discussion when the opportunity arises. If this is the case, tell your partner you have something important to discuss, and then, have your discussion. When it comes to important topics, such as running the house or caring for other family members, your partner deserves to have a say in what happens.

Tamsen's Tip

There have been times when I could not contact my husband to talk to him about something important before making a decision, so I would send an email to explain to him what happened and why I made the decision I did. I always tried to take into account what he would do in a similar situation if he were the one making the decision on my behalf.

Sharing finances while apart

Not all couples share finances, so if you are not yet to a point in your relationship where this is a shared consideration, then keep in mind that there might come a time when you decide to combine finances. When that time comes, approach the situation with open communication and willingness to compromise when necessary. Money can be a heated topic, especially if this is a topic you and your partner have not talked about previously. You might have one idea of how money should be handled while your partner has a different idea, and when you realize you do not see eye to eye, it can be disconcerting.

Whether you and your partner share the duty of managing the finances depends on your situation and preferences. In some instances, it is obvious who should manage the household budget; it is impractical to assume that one person will manage the money if that person will not have time to make sure the bills get paid. Financial radio talk show host Dave Ramsey suggests that a couple should work together to manage the household finances, but when they do not live under the same roof (some or all the time), it can become exponentially more difficult to manage finances together. On the other hand, it is not an impossible task. Sharing the burden of managing the household finances, despite being apart, can strengthen the relationship. Having to work together to solve money issues and make long-term financial decisions is another way to promote the "we are in this together" mentality that strong relationships have.

Compose a budget together. This might turn out to be one master budget with a sub-budget for each of you while apart. Start by figuring out how much money you cumulatively bring in, and then figure out how much your monthly financial obligations are. If there is not much money left over, figure out ways to cut expenses or bring in more income. Working together will help put the two of you on the same page. Examples of items that should be listed on your budget include housing expenses, utilities, credit card and loan payments, gas for your cars, insurance, entertainment funds, and any other recurring expenses. Think about what you spend your money on each month.

How you manage the finances together will look different depending on your circumstances. No matter what the situation, if you share accounts jointly, then there should be communication about money.

If the burden of managing finances falls on your shoulders, here are some tips:

- Keep lines of communication open with your partner. If feasible, run financial decisions past your partner so there can be an open dialogue about the decisions being made.

- Get help. There are books and software programs that will guide you along the path to managing your money effectively. If you need additional help, seek out a financial planner or other money professional. It is better to get help than to flounder around with household finances. *The Appendix at the end of this book has resources that can help.*

- Consider opening up "fun" deposit accounts for you and your partner. These can be accounts with a weekly or monthly amount deposited to use however the person wants to spend it. This allows both of you to have some money to use for small purchases and not have to "report" back to the other person. Prepaid cards work well for this purpose, too; if your partner visits Starbucks® twice a day, a prepaid Starbucks card reloaded with monthly funds can simplify things.

- Hiding purchases or lying about finances is not good for a relationship, but the problems arising from these instances can be even more harmful in a long-distance relationship. Suppose your partner discovers you have been indulging in shopping sprees and, at the same time, you have been urging your partner to curb spending. This situation could make your partner wonder what else you have been hiding. When trust is severely damaged in a long-distance relationship, it can be the beginning of the end.

When you do not share finances, which is common with couples who are not married or who do not live under the same roof, it is still good to talk about money to make sure you are on the same page. Talking about things, such as credit scores, saving account balances, and debt is not romantic, but if this is the person you are going to spend the rest of your life with, or even if you are just thinking about it, then these discussions are important.

Money and emotion

Spending can be tied to emotions, and for many people, higher levels of stress or sadness can result in an increase in spending, particularly on nonessential items. If you are sad that your partner is away, or you are feeling lonely without your partner, you might find that you start to fill the void of your partner with other things. Although there is nothing wrong with occasional splurges as long as your budget can allow the spending, if you find that spending money has become your main source of entertainment, you will want to make a conscious effort to reign in the spending so you do not wind up causing lasting damage to your finances.

Tamsen's Tip

During my husband's year-long military assignment overseas, I got into the habit of visiting my favorite clothing store a couple of times a week. It took me awhile to realize that I was turning to shopping to fill the void of my husband being gone, but the realization certainly hit when my closet was so stuffed with clothes that I could not fit anything else in it. I cancelled my credit card with the clothing store and started monitoring my spending a lot more closely.

Being in a long-distance relationship can be expensive. Phone bills, airline tickets, and gifts to send back and forth can add up quickly, and before you know it, you might find yourself in a financial mess. You probably have the desire to connect with your partner, so you justify the expensive phone bill. You justify putting airline tickets or rental cars on your credit card even though you really cannot afford it because you miss your partner so much. You send flowers or other gifts to your partner in an attempt to show affection, but you do this so much that the bills start to pile up.

Although it is certainly understandable that you might justify these purchases in your mind, try to look at the bigger picture overall. A relationship that has to deal with the underlying problem of massive debt is going to have a difficult time flourishing.

It might feel good to splurge, and you might be able to justify these purchases in your mind because of your situation away from your partner, but in the long term, it is not a good idea to spend with reckless abandon.

Try to find ways to connect with your partner that do not necessarily involve spending money. Look to less expensive alternatives when the time does come to make a purchase. Instead of sending a dozen red roses, send some less expensive flowers. If you have to buy airline tickets, shop around for the most reasonable prices and be flexible with your travel dates. Just because there is emotion attached to your purchases, it does not mean that your purchases have to be impulsive. Think things through, and try to get the best deal possible. Your long-distance relationship has a far better chance of flourishing if the two of you are not worried about how to pay the credit card bill this month.

Raising children

Anyone who raises children will tell you it is a tough, yet rewarding job. Add to this the fact that one person is largely responsible for raising the children while the other partner is away, and the rewarding job becomes even tougher. If you have children, or if you are planning to have children, it is important to realize that long-distance arrangements can have a huge impact on the children, too. You already know it can be difficult for your partner to be away from you, but imagine how this must feel to children who have to deal with one parent away and one parent at home.

Be on the same page with your partner when it comes to raising children. Your discipline tactics, chore expectations, and other important parenting factors should be in sync with what your partner expects you to do. You might not agree on everything, but the way you deal with your children should not be a shock to your partner. Partners can experience strong feelings about raising children in a long-distance relationship. The parent left to raise the children might feel an unfair burden has been placed on his or her shoulders while the parent who is away might feel helpless and absent. When one parent starts deviating from the agreement on how to raise the children without first talking it through with the other parent, this can make the distance feel even further and become a major source of frustration. Add to this the confusion for children that can result from an unpredictable parent, and this can be a bad situation.

Tamsen's Tip

Sometimes, we follow different rules in our house when my husband is gone. Bedtime tends to be a lot earlier, mainly because I need time at night to work. Saturdays become "Mommy Sleeps In Day," and the kids are allowed to indulge in a cereal of their choosing as long as they prepare their own breakfasts and wait until after 8 a.m. to wake me up. The reason this all works — and does not wind up making my husband feel as though all the rules are changing when he is gone — is because I keep him up to date on how I am running things while he is gone.

Things can change, however. Discipline tactics must evolve along with the cognitive sophistication of the child, and as new challenges arise, parents have to adjust. The important thing is to keep the lines of communication open between you and your partner. It is also important to give children the opportunity to communicate with the parent who is away when possible. Whether that takes the form of writing letters, talking on the phone, or using the computer to communicate, children need to know the parent who is away is still present in their lives. Do not allow the relationship between children and the parent who is away to dwindle and deteriorate.

Tamsen's Tip

Children are resilient. It might not be the ideal situation to have a parent who is away, but as long as the away parent makes it clear that he or she still loves the children and makes them feel valued, they can deal with the situation. If your child does not seem to be coping well with a parent away, especially if the parent is in a potentially dangerous situation, seek counseling for your child. Sometimes, having a neutral adult to talk to can help children immensely.

Further complications can arise when it comes to raising children while in a long-distance relationship. The key is to figure out ways to make day-to-day tasks as simple as possible for everyone involved. For example, if the child has medical issues that require intensive effort from the parent at home, look into respite care or actively seek out help from friends and family. If you are a step-parent who suddenly has to take care of children solo despite not knowing them well or never having dealt with children — such as might be the case for a newlywed military couple — seek out help from seasoned parents and allow yourself mistakes as you grow into the new role. The recurring theme is to seek out help. Surround yourself with people you can trust and people who are willing to help you. *You will learn more about surrounding yourself with the right people in Chapter 6.*

A parent away is still a parent. The parent at home should not disregard the feelings of the parent away, just as the parent away should not switch off the feeling of responsibility for his or her children. Parenthood can be tough, but it also can be a huge problem in a long-distance relationship if the parents disagree about how to handle parenthood or if one parent "checks out" and leaves the burden of raising the children to the other part-ner completely. You can be away and still be an excellent parent, especially if you continually offer support to your partner and make an effort to make sure your children know you adore them.

Being a solo parent

If you are used to having the help of a partner, even if that help is limited to after your partner gets off work, you probably will find being a parent on your own while your partner is away is an entirely different world. Although the level of difficulty has a lot to do with the age of your children, trying to parent solo when you are used to having some help from a partner can be incredibly difficult.

You will have to give yourself plenty of grace when it comes to your parenting. You might be the type of parent who never lets your young kids watch television, but a week or two into your partner being gone, you might break down and flip on the TV for your kids so you can get a break. Or you might be the type of parent who would never think of going through a drive-thru for dinner, but after a long day when you know there is no help waiting for you at home with the kids, a drive-thru starts to sound like the perfect solution to your dinner dilemma. Giving in to these types of whims does not make you a bad parent, especially if these new behaviors do not become the norm for your parenting. Tell the kids that you are doing these things as a special treat, and they will not expect them all the time. Tell your partner what you are doing if it is something the two of you need

to discuss, particularly if you have both agreed upon a certain way of raising the kids, and you find yourself deviating from that plan (for example, allowing the children to watch television if this is something you and your partner were both adamantly against at one point).

Do not allow feelings of exhaustion while parenting solo to evolve into feelings of resentment toward your partner. Parenting can be tedious, but parenting solo when you are accustomed to parenting with your partner can be unlike anything you have ever done. This is especially true for people who do not have family members or friends nearby who can give them breaks occasionally or for people who cannot afford to splurge on occasional babysitters for some time away. So, although you do not want to censor the difficulty you encounter being a solo parent while talking to your partner on the phone or via email, you also do not want to allow your heightened stress levels to explode into an angry tirade unleashed upon your unsuspecting partner. There is nothing wrong with telling your partner that handling the parenting duties alone is hard — in fact, if this is the case, then you certainly want to share things with your partner, so you are not candy coating what is going on at home while he or she is away. But make sure you do not resort to resenting your partner for not being the one to stay home to care for the children.

In the meantime, do what you can to help your children get through this rough time and keep your partner up to date on what is going on with the entire family. Most important, take care of yourself, and remember that though parenting is an incredibly important role — perhaps one of the most important roles you will ever have in your life — there is more to you than the person who takes care of everyone else. Take care of yourself, too, so you will have the energy to care for the children, and your partner will not come home to an utterly exhausted person on the verge of a nervous breakdown.

Other responsibilities

Who is going to send Aunt Mary her birthday card? Who will visit Uncle Brandon in the hospital? Who is going to pull together the receipts for taxes? When a couple physically lives together, these small questions resolve themselves naturally as one partner takes the lead in taking care of everyday tasks. But when the couple does not live under the same roof, even the smallest tasks can turn into big issues.

It can be helpful to develop a list or schedule of the tasks that need to be completed on a regular basis and to assign responsibility for those tasks. Your relationship might not even be at a point where you need to worry about composing a list of duties because you are dating someone who lives far away. On the other hand, if you are in a committed relationship with someone who spends time away, a list of assigned responsibilities will be beneficial. The amount of tasks listed on the schedule will vary depending on the couple. One couple might be content with one person handling all the household responsibilities while another couple might have a complicated roster of responsibilities that are managed by both people in tandem. A couple with children, a mortgage, a business, and a dog will have a more complex list than other couples with more simplified lives. On the other hand, both couples can benefit from a clear division of responsibilities while living apart.

Be reasonable. If your partner is in no position to take care of these tasks, pick up the slack, and do them. All too often, one member of a long-distance couple will feel as though too many burdens fall upon his or her shoulders, and though this might be true, these tasks have to be done. Consider an example where one partner is home, and the other partner has accepted a one-year contract to work overseas. The partner left at home has increased responsibilities during the other partner's absence because the partner overseas is in no position to schedule doctor appointments, to shop for birthday gifts for the children, or to run around town trying to find the best prices for new tires for the car. Even if it is not necessarily fair that the partner left at home has increased responsibilities, it is the reality of the situation. If you are the partner who has the burden of responsibility, consider it an opportunity to take control of the situation, and do what you have to do. If you are the partner who has left the responsibilities with the other person, be sure to express gratitude for your partner's extra work. Otherwise, you might find your relationship in a situation where one partner feels unappreciated, and the other partner feels helpless because things are not getting done at home, as they should.

Communication is the key to avoiding a host of problems in a long-distance relationship. Make sure each partner has a defined role in the relationship, and leave wiggle room for that role to evolve as circumstances change. Your relationship might not have issues such as these because you do not share a household and, therefore, do not share everyday responsibilities, but if you anticipate someday consolidating your households into one while still maintaining a long-distance relationship, start to think now about how duties will be split. Clear communication regarding expectations for each person's role and duties can save grief later.

Not every long-distance relationship encounters this situation because not all relationships involve a shared household, but if you do, do not become resentful for the extra work necessary to maintain a household while your partner is away. If you are the one who is away and cannot tackle these duties, do not take your partner for granted or develop resentment about not having control over what happens at home. *You will learn more about dealing with resentment in a long-distance relationship in Chapter 6.*

Asking for help

You already turn to certain people for help. Friends, family, and even paid folks, such as housecleaning services or other helpers, can ease the stress involved with having a partner away. Some people find it difficult to ask for help or to accept unsolicited offers of help even when their partners are not around. On the other hand, if you have a trusted circle of people around you, ask for — and accept — help. Perhaps someone wants to help you change the oil in your car or take you out for coffee and conversation because you seem to be under stress; whatever the offer of help, it should not be dismissed involuntarily because you want to be able to do it all on your own while your partner is away.

It is all right to turn to your partner for help. Just because your partner is not physically with you, it does not mean that you should censor yourself and not ask for help or support from him or her. When you present only the positive parts of your life to your long-distance partner, you are not presenting the entire truth. There is nothing wrong with turning to your partner for support even though he or she is not there with you. Doing so might bring the two of you even closer. Your partner might feel bad or helpless about not being there physically to support you, so when you ask for advice or help from your partner, you are helping him or her feel like an important person in your life.

However, there is a fine line between asking for help and whining about every problem you encounter. In the previous section, you were urged to not complain about the burden that might be placed on you because of your partner's absence. Although this is decent advice, you also do not want to do the opposite and not utter a word about any problems or challenges. This is not a realistic portrayal of your life.

What help should you ask of your partner while you are apart? Ask for things your partner is capable of helping with, or if you are looking for advice or a listening ear, make that clear. If you provide your partner with an expectation of what you want, make it clear how he or she can help you from miles away.

Right: "My to-do list is overwhelming me. Would you be willing to go online and send flowers to Marlene? She will be in the hospital for the next few days for that procedure I told you about."

Wrong: "It kills me that you cannot go visit Marlene in the hospital. I bet she would love to see you. She will be crushed when nobody can go see her. As for me, I have so much to do that I doubt I will even get to send her flowers or anything."

In the first example, the person speaking admits that he or she could use some help and then offers the possible solution. Also, the person had already mentioned Marlene's medical procedure, which means that the lines of communication are open between the couple. In the second example, the person blurts out unrealistic expectations of the other person and delivers a swift guilt trip. The person mentions the problem at hand but does not specifically ask the other person to handle the task.

The first example is preferable for more than one reason, but the best aspect of this approach is that the other person is able to see what task can be taken and how this will help his or her partner. This would not be an ideal example if the other person had no way to access the Internet to order flowers or did not have the financial means to buy flowers. The example only works if the first person that presented the solution knows it is something the second person is capable of managing.

Take note: Carefully watch your words, and only ask your partner what you know he or she can accomplish. Be genuine when talking to your partner, and do not be afraid to ask for help as long as you know your partner can give you the help for which you are looking. For example, ask your partner who resides in another state to do comparison shopping online for your next car purchase, but do not ask the same of a partner who is in a combat zone overseas and has little to no access to the Internet.

Tamsen's Tip

The help you can get from a partner who is away might surprise you. I once mentioned to my deployed husband that I needed to hire someone to trim the hedges in our front yard, and the next day I awoke to the sounds of someone in our front yard trimming hedges. My husband had emailed a man from our church to ask if he would be willing to do yard work for us, and he was happy to oblige. My husband had solved the problem without me even asking or expecting him to.

What if you are the type of person who is self-sufficient and does not like to ask for help? If this is the case, stay true to who you are because this is who your partner wants you to be. Do not fabricate errands or tasks to give to your partner in an attempt to make him or her feel more useful while away. However, give your partner opportunities to give you advice, whether it is advice on how to approach a difficult situation at work or which restaurant to visit. By doing this, you allow your partner to feel as though he or she is still a part of your everyday life, even if you do not get to see each other often.

Get creative if your partner tells you about a problem or issue that needs to be resolved. It is amazing what can be done over the Internet, so if your partner talks about needing to find something or hire a service, hop online, and do the work for him or her. Taking work off your partner's hands is helpful and is a gesture that shows you care.

Chapter 3

Communication is the Key

One thing needs to be perfectly clear: Communication is a make-it-or-break-it factor in a long-distance relationship. This is not to say that limited communication will lead to the demise of your relationship or that constant communication will guarantee a life of eternal love together. What it means is if you want to flourish in your long-distance relationship, you and your partner must place communication high on your list of priorities.

Communication looks different for every long-distance couple and depends on a variety of factors. Being in a long-distance relationship does not doom you to having less-than-stellar communication. Some couples live under the same roof yet do not spend time communicating. You can be in a long-distance relationship and still manage to have excellent communication with your partner, even if you hardly ever see each other in person.

This does not mean you and your partner have to speak to each other every day. It means the quality of your communication matters over the quantity. It will not help to chat with your partner for hours about the color you want to paint your bedroom walls when what you want to say is, "I feel lonely and need to know you still care about me."

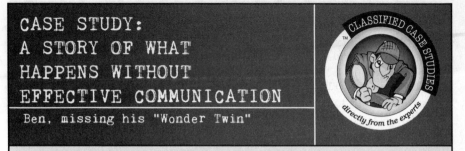

CASE STUDY:
A STORY OF WHAT
HAPPENS WITHOUT
EFFECTIVE COMMUNICATION

Ben, missing his "Wonder Twin"

In 2008, my marriage ended with a grinding halt. Everything I knew and owned swiftly was pulled out from underneath me: my beautiful Las Vegas home, my recording studio, my investments, my children, and my sanity. With nothing left, I ventured back to my native Boise, Idaho, to rebuild. Through the sparkling rise of Facebook, I began reconnecting with people from my past, which was therapeutic in my divorce recovery. That is how I found Michelle (name changed), a woman from my past.

Come to find out that she, too, had been through a divorce and some other ugly dating relationships. For a few months, we periodically talked on the phone and slowly realized that the core of who we were had never changed. That was the one thing that drew us to each other so many years before. One day in late November, I was having a conversation with Michelle over the phone and asked her what she was doing for Christmas. She replied that she did not have any plans, and on a whim, I asked her to come spend Christmas with me. I never thought in a million years that she would take me up on the offer, but she did. When she showed up on my doorstep, it seemed like time had stopped. She was as beautiful as I remembered, and we just got to know each other again. The first night, we stayed up until 3 a.m. talking over wine and catching up. I was at peace because I got to hold her after almost 20 years.

The next day, she returned home, and we parted with a simple hug — no kisses or anything further. I remember how I could not stop thinking about her; day and night, she was on my mind. Rather than coming off like a person with a stalker personality, I went and bought a journal. I wrote in a the journal daily telling her what was going on in my daily life and how much I missed her and thought of her. I always ended my daily entries with, "I adore you." The reason, which I later explained to her, was because people constantly say "I love you" superficially, and each human interprets love differently. I have not heard the same definition from two people. "I adore you" can only be taken in the context for which it is spoken. It is an absolute that cannot be misrepresented.

I wrote, not knowing when I would see Michelle again. Luckily, in March, she was going to Las Vegas for the first time for a photo convention. During a phone conversation, I agreed to come to Vegas and show her around in the proper fashion. I still had several connections and took full advantage of it. A little nervous, I also introduced my children to her. My kids have been exposed to several new relationships in which their mother is constantly involved. So, like their father, they, too, are sketchy when it comes to trust. This was not the case with Michelle. Instantly, my children bonded with her, and I knew she was the one.

Later that night, Michelle explained to me that she was nervous about getting involved in another relationship but loved where we were going together. She and I shared identical ideals and commonly referred to the other as "My Wonder Twin." We were perfect for each other. I presented her with the journal and told her how much I cared for her. In a Hollywood romance moment, we were close to kissing, and she said, "I'm scared." I leaned into her and said, "Quit being such a chicken," and kissed her. It was magic. I had been waiting to do this for too long. I had my Wonder Twin, and my children adored her.

The biggest problem was that I did not know when I was going to get to see her next because of our busy schedules. At the end of May, her birthday was rapidly approaching. Her best friend "Julie" (name changed) contacted me via Facebook and informed me that she was planning a surprise birthday party and wanted me there. I warned Julie that Michelle absolutely hated surprises and advised against it. Julie insisted, and so I played along. All the while, I kept writing in a new journal. Michelle and I spoke about three times a week or more and sent text messages as well. I knew that if I were patient, things would fall into place.

Michelle's birthday came, and I booked a room at the same hotel where everyone else was staying. I made plans, drove nearly five hours to her town, and met up with her friends, none of whom I had ever met. As we hid for the surprise, Michelle and Julie made their entrance. Michelle was fighting back her anger (remember she hates surprises), but when she noticed I was there, she came and gave me a big hug. Later in the evening, I received a phone call from my management so I went outside, and Michelle left the room to get some fresh air. She came to me and said, "Thank you for coming. I would lose my mind right now if you were not here." What was hardest for me during the party was the amount of men that showed up, as if they were all dating her. I quietly sat in the background observing. After the evening was over, Michelle followed me to my room and explained to me that I was the one she wanted to be next to, and that I was the one she had waited all night to kiss. My nervous trust issues were now set at ease.

A few weeks later, my children came to spend the summer with me, and Michelle came to stay with us for a week. Again, I felt complete. I told Michelle that "everything I cared about is in this room." We also talked a lot about if we were to get married that our vows would be so full of emotion that our poor guests would suffer. The possibility of us being together forever looked very promising.

Over the next few months, we continued to see each other. Then, I started to notice pictures of her on Facebook that caused me to be skeptical. She was going to photography seminars and would often be in pictures with other men. I told her how this affected my soul. I had terrible trust issues, and she was the one thing I adored more than anything on earth.

We had several conversations, and one that struck me hard was when she told me I was acting like a jealous control freak, like her ex-husband. I quickly apologized, but things began to rapidly change. I felt unimportant and started seeing someone else. To my fault, I did not officially tell Michelle it was over. Somewhere in the back of my mind, I think I wanted her to come rushing back to me. On Valentine's Day, she figured out I was involved in a new relationship. I felt awful (and I still do) that I did not discuss it with her. Little did I know that she too was writing me a journal (one I have not seen to this day) and that I made her feel she was not enough. I have not felt so terrible in my entire life. In my mind, I felt like I had committed adultery, and I did. Shame on me for thinking with my brain instead of my heart. I let my "Wonder Twin" slip through my fingers and out of my life. My prayer is that she would forgive me and see me for who I am. I miss her.

Communication Will Make or Break a Relationship

The next time you have a conversation with someone face-to-face, pay attention to how much of the conversation is never spoken. So much communication is exchanged in a nonverbal way, whether it is a roll of the eyes or tensing of the body. People might say things their body language contradicts, and often, the nonverbal communication is the most accurate portrayal of the person's true feelings.

This is one of the reasons why communication in a long-distance relationship can be tough. When communication is reduced largely to email, texts, and phone calls, words and meanings might be misinterpreted. Suppose one person sends a text to his or her partner that says, "I wish I could be there for you the way your friends are." Depending on the context in which this text was sent and the way the recipient interprets this text, there could be myriad meanings behind what the text means.

The sender might have meant:

- "I appreciate that your friend was able to help you out when you needed a ride to the post office. I sometimes feel guilty that I cannot be there to help you, but it helps me feel better knowing there are other people who care about you and are willing to help you. We are lucky to have such friends."

- "I miss you, and I wish I was near you all the time. I would trade places with your friends if I could so I could hug you and see you."

- "I am resentful because you constantly complain that I am not there for you like your friends are. You already know that I cannot physically be there for you, but you continue to complain about it. Unfortunately, I cannot be there for you, and I wish you would stop complaining about it."

- "I think you are cheating on me with someone you claim is only a friend. I think it started because you were lonely and wanted someone to talk to, so you turned to this friend. I do not have proof though, so instead of blatantly accusing you of having an affair, I am going to drop passive-aggressive hints and hope this prompts you to tell me the truth."

The recipient of the text does not have the advantage of seeing the sender's body language during this interaction, nor is the recipient even able to listen to the tone of voice of the sender. It is easy to tell when someone says something with the intention of portraying verbal irony; in this instance, if the sentence were said with a sneer, it would be obvious in the speaker's tone of voice. Text or email takes away the advantage of scrutinizing the other cues present beyond the face value of what the words are saying.

When your relationship is long distance, your communication with your partner will be via methods that are not face-to-face. There is also a chance you will not have the opportunity to communicate with your partner as much as you would like. When two people live in separate places, they have separate lives even if they are a couple. Much to the chagrin of the two people involved in a long-distance relationship, communication has to take a back seat to daily life.

Staying together when apart

Communication is important in any relationship, but when a relationship is long distance, communication might be one of the only ways the couple can stay connected. There are no flirtatious glances, quick squeezes of the hand, or opportunities to surprise each other with breakfast in bed when a couple has to live separately. These little things that serve as reminders that they enjoy a special connection are largely absent in a long-distance relationship, which makes communication more important. Think of communication as a way to stay connected.

A long-distance relationship is not going to thrive if there is little or no communication, especially if there was not a solid foundation for the couple in the beginning. Even the strongest relationships can suffer if communication is not sufficient when separated. Consider military families, in which one member of the couple has to go away for months and has limited communication with the other partner. Even if the couple has a strong bond to begin with, and even if they are in love with each other, the length of time with limited communication can cause an emotional distance that can turn into big problems if the couple is not able to reconnect when they are together again. This is why the military offers and promotes counseling to couples before and after deployments; lack of communication causes issues, even with couples who do not have any other major problems.

Think of communication as a vital and necessary aspect to any long-distance relationship. Search for ways to keep communication open, and if necessary, cater to the communication styles that best suit both of you. For example, there are people who are eloquent in writing yet feel awkward when speaking on the telephone. There are people who would rather visit the dentist than sit in front of a computer and have a video chat session. Respect your partner's preferences when it comes to communicating, but make sure you also make your own preferences clear. Your partner might hate texting, but if you feel most loved when your partner sends a text or two a day to show that he or she is thinking about you, make it clear that you appreciate the effort it takes your partner to send those daily texts. You also might feel an elevated sense of closeness with a partner who is willing to step outside his or her comfort zone to make you feel special.

Set clear expectations for communication in your long-distance relationship. If you expect your partner to call you every night to wish you sweet dreams — and if it is feasible for your partner to do this — let your partner know that this is your expectation and is something you will expect unless your partner tells you otherwise. Your partner might not even realize the vital importance of these phone calls to wish you sweet dreams, so the first time your partner forgets to call before going to sleep, you might panic and think this must be a sign your relationship is deteriorating. In reality, your partner just fell asleep before calling and did not realize this would cause such an emotional upheaval for you.

Do you see how this scenario quickly might evolve into a huge fight? You call your partner demanding to know why you did not receive your nighttime phone call, and your partner is so taken aback by your emotional outburst that he or she reciprocates by saying you are too controlling. Your partner does not understand why he or she is suddenly getting reprimanded. You cherish the nightly telephone calls, and you were hurt when you did not get your call, but emotions can cloud the truth when communication is not open and honest.

If you have any hope of flourishing in a long-distance relationship, one thing is essential: Do not expect your partner to be able to read your mind. Communicate how you feel and what you expect. Although some partners might be able to notice subtle hints regarding what the other partner wants based on nonverbal communication, you do not have this advantage when involved with someone long distance. If you want a nightly phone call, tell your partner that. Do not hint that you want a nightly phone call, complain that you feel particularly lonely before bed, or just not say anything and brood silently about how your partner cannot sense you want to receive a phone call every night. This is not fair to you, and it is not fair to your partner.

Communication does not come easily for everyone. You or your partner might have grown accustomed to not speaking your mind or saying things just to placate everyone else. This is common with people who have a desire to please everyone or who do not feel confident enough to reveal what they want and expect. Some people do not know what they want, so they do not feel they are in any position to tell other people what they want. Being in a long-distance relationship is not the time to keep your feelings to yourself. If anything, be more verbal and clear about what you want and what you expect from your partner.

Questions to ask yourself and your partner

Ask yourself these questions to prepare yourself to communicate more effectively with your long-distance partner, and then ask your partner to answer the questions, too. You might be surprised by the answers.

- When do I feel most loved?

- When do I feel most vulnerable?

- What are the best ways for my partner to demonstrate love and affection from afar?

- What are some deal breakers for this relationship? Deal breakers are things that you cannot put up with that would likely cause the end of the relationship.

- What is my favorite form of communication with my partner?

- What is my least favorite form of communication with my partner, and how can I make it more enjoyable?

- Am I a decent communicator?

- Do I sometimes say things that I do not mean?

- What can I do to improve communication in my long-distance relationship?

The act of communicating comes easily to most people. The majority of people do not have trouble calling a pizza place to order a delivery or conveying to a friend what a movie was about. Communication can get tricky when emotions are involved, and the trickiness increases when the person you are talking to is hardly ever around. Consider communication in your long-distance relationship to be important and worthy of working on to ensure you have the best communication possible with your partner. It might be the thing that takes your long-distance relationship from a maybe-forever status to a definite-forever status.

Quick Tips for Making Communication a Priority

Making sure communication is a priority in your long-distance relationship does not have to be a daunting task, especially if you and your partner seem to be on the same page with most things. You already might have a rapport with your partner that allows both of you to speak your mind and clearly state what your expectations are. If this is the case, you just might need to work on staying connected and keeping communication open. If, on the other hand, you and your partner routinely misinterpret each other and find that mixed communication is a recurring theme in your arguments, then make a concerted effort to improve your communication to give your long-distance relationship a chance to flourish.

Convey your needs

If you have ever wished that your partner knew how you felt or what you were thinking, take solace in the fact that you are not the only person with that wish. The easy way to remedy this problem is to open up communication and tell your partner how you feel and what you are thinking.

Do you want your partner to tell you that you are attractive? Instead of hinting around, tell your partner it means something to you when he or she tells you how attractive you are. If all else fails, ask your partner, "Do you think I am attractive?" It is not fishing for a compliment but, instead, getting what you need to feel secure in your relationship.

Discover your partner's needs

You might have at one point wished you could crawl into your partner's head and figure out what was going through his or her brain. You do not have to resort to such measures when you ask what is going on. Although your partner might not be comfortable sharing every detail of his or her thoughts, the fact that you care enough to ask — and listen to the answer — fosters an open communication environment in the relationship.

Avoid communication overdose

Communication is important in a long-distance relationship, but so is being cognizant of your partner's feelings. You do not have to describe every detail of your trip to the grocery store, especially if you have limited time to spend on the phone or computer with your partner. If you talk or write too much, your partner might start to tune you out. Do not fall into the trap of communicating just for the sake of communicating. In other words, know what bores your partner, and avoid it. If you are not sure what bores your partner, ask. If the two of you have open communication, this should be an enlightening conversation. On the other hand, if you are reluctant to ask your partner to list what topics bore him or her, or if you are pretty sure that your partner would care more about sparing your feelings instead of telling you the truth about what topics are boring, pay attention to your partner's reactions. Use your observations to figure out what topics seem to make your partner lose interest. Does your partner start mumbling "uh-huh" a lot when you start talking about your favorite sports team? Does your partner seem distracted when the topic of your knitting hobby comes into the conversation? These are relatively reliable indications that you have lost your partner's interest.

Tamsen's Tip

My husband calls my loss of interest in a conversation "Tamsen's Power Save." He says that he can always tell when I have lost interest because I appear to go on power save, just like a laptop that has been sitting unused for a few minutes. Instead of getting offended by my lack of interest, we have a good laugh.

Jump over communication hurdles

If you never get face-to-face time with your partner to talk, use a telephone. If you or your partner does not have ready access to a telephone, use email. If phone and email are not options, communicate the old-fashioned way and resort to written letters sent through the mail. Communication should be a priority in your long-distance relationship. Do not allow a hurdle to stop you from communicating with your partner.

Adjust as needed

Do not be afraid to try new ways of communicating. As technology evolves, so do the methods available for staying in touch with people far away. If you are not a fan of one particular method of communicating, let your partner know how you feel and suggest alternatives for staying in touch. Be aware of your partner's preferences for communication as well. You do not want to disregard one method of communication completely if it is your partner's favorite way of talking to you.

Tamsen's Tip

I am not the biggest fan of video chat when the Internet connection is slow, as is the case sometimes when chatting online with someone in an overseas location. I prefer instant messaging, and luckily, my husband understands the frustration I feel when sitting through a bad connection on video chat does not help our communication.

Keep communication center stage

Some people grow accustomed to their long-distance relationship and forget to work at staying connected to their partner. Periodically review the communication between you and your partner. Are you both covering important things when you talk? Are you conveying your genuine feelings to your partner, while also asking to hear about his or her genuine feelings? Do not allow communication to fall by the wayside.

Communication includes listening

Communication is not all about telling your partner how you feel; it is also about listening to the things your partner says. This does not mean waiting for your partner to finish talking, so you swiftly can move on to the next thing you want to talk about. This means truly listening to your partner and understanding the things he or she says. There is a chance this is what you expect from your partner, so follow suit, and give your partner the same respect in communication.

Active listening

Listening is crucial in a long-distance relationship, but it becomes even more important when the two of you are having a serious discussion or an argument. Active listening involves acknowledging what your partner has said before moving on with what

you want to say. This ensures you actually understood the meaning of what your partner was trying to convey instead of hearing something else entirely. When communication takes place via telephone or email, it can be difficult to glean the actual meaning of what your partner is trying to get across. It becomes even more difficult when you are trying to discuss something emotional or something you do not necessarily agree on. Your interpretation of what your partner is trying to say might be skewed by what you *think* your partner is trying to say.

Here is an example of a typical conversation, followed by how active listening might help clarify the conversation for the two people involved.

Person 1: *I cannot believe you forgot about our lunch date.*

Person 2: *I cannot be at your beck and call.*

Person 1: *We made these plans weeks ago! You never have time for me.*

Person 2: *I have to work! I cannot just drop everything and scamper off to lunch with you when I have work to do.*

Here is the same conversation, but with active listening, there is a better chance that this conversation will not end in one or both partners walking away from the conversation angry.

Person 1: *I cannot believe that you forgot about our lunch date.*

Person 2: *I hear you saying that you are upset that I forgot about our lunch date.*

Person 1: *Yes, that is what I am saying.*

Person 2: *I understand that you are upset. I am sorry that I upset you because that is not what I intended.*

Person 1: *I hear you apologizing, and I appreciate the apology.*

Person 2: *I want you to understand that work has been really hectic for me lately, and I feel a lot of pressure from you to follow whatever schedule you put into place for me.*

Person 1: *So, you are saying that I put too much pressure on you? I just want to have time with you.*

Person 2: *I know that you want to spend time with me. I am not saying that I do not want to spend time with you. Instead, I am saying that I need a little more leeway nowadays with my hectic work schedule.*

Person 1: *I hear you saying that you do want to spend time with me, but I need to try to be flexible with my demands on your time. Is that right?*

Person 2: *Yes, that is what I am trying to say. Please understand that I really do want to spend time with you. I feel horrible about forgetting our lunch date.*

Person 1: *I want to spend time with you too. How about you look at your schedule and let me know when lunch will work with your schedule?*

Person 2: *That sounds great.*

Active listening can sound a little robotic or scripted, but it is not a technique to be used all the time. This is a common technique used by couples counselors to ensure both people involved in the conversation get their points across successfully before moving along in the conversation. It allows both people to clarify points as necessary, and nobody walks away from the conversation wondering what the other person was saying. It also keeps the emotional response to a minimum because both people in the conversation are forced to be logical and analytical. Try using the active listening technique the next time you have to discuss something sensitive with your partner. When serious conversations have to take place from a distance, helping techniques like active listening can make the conversation go much more smoothly.

"I" versus "You"

A common mistake couples make when having heated conversations is to shift the focus off "I" and onto "You." For example, instead of saying "I am hurt because you forgot our lunch date," you might say, "You do not care about me enough to remember our lunch date." Instead of effectively conveying your feelings, this results in you forcing the blame onto your partner while also attacking his or her commitment to you. It is one thing to be upset that your partner forgot about your lunch date, but it is another thing entirely to accuse your partner of not caring about you. Even if there is truth to the accusation of your partner not caring about you as much as you would like, focus on the topic at hand, and deal with the bigger problems when the time is right.

One of the easiest ways to make sure your conversation stays on topic is to start your sentences with the phrase "I feel." This will keep you from attacking your partner while also giving you the opportunity to get your point across. So, instead of "If you cared about me you would have made time for me," it instead becomes, "I feel hurt that you forgot about our lunch date." The second sentence directly addresses your feelings and gives your partner the opportunity to respond. The first sentence has the potential to allow the conversation to veer off in an unattended direction, never really allowing the actual problem to get resolved or even addressed.

You cannot assume what your partner is feeling. Do not tell your partner that his or her feelings are invalid because feelings often are emotionally driven and hard to define to begin with. Saying something to your partner along the lines of "Your feelings are wrong" can be a damaging statement. Focus on your own feelings and effectively conveying those feelings to your partner in your conversation. Combine this technique with the effective listening techniques, and your difficult conversations can be productive and resolved even when you cannot have the conversation face-to-face.

Absolutes

One more important thing to remember when trying to effectively communicate with your partner is to avoid absolute statements. Absolutes refer to words like "never" or "always." For example, if you tell your partner he or she never listens to you, you are putting an absolute within your claim that invalidates the entire statement. It cannot be true that your partner never listens to you. If it were true, what would be the point in making the statement in the first place?

When you make an absolute statement, what you are actually trying to convey is something emphatic. You emphatically believe that in some instances, your partner does not listen to what you say. Although this might be true, it is certainly not the same as making the statement that your partner never listens to you. When you put it in absolute terms, you lose your credibility in the assertion. Your partner will not hear your feelings or frustrations in that statement; instead, your partner will hear only the accusation. Do not be surprised if this elicits an angry response from your partner.

When having a serious discussion or argument with your partner, avoid absolutes because they are seldom true. Do not mask absolutes in discussions of your feelings, either. In other words, just because you start the sentence "you never listen to me" with "I feel," it does not make it any more effective when trying to resolve the issue. Instead, say, "I feel as though there are some times when you do not listen to me," which is probably much more accurate than "You never listen to me."

Arguments happen

You are not going to be able to avoid arguments altogether. *You will learn more about fighting fairly later in this chapter.* When you are in a long-distance relationship, the need for effective communication becomes even more important, so you can both feel as though you are on the same page despite the distance. Although it might feel odd to bring communication tools into heated conversations, the result is a more constructive conversation that builds the connection between the two of you. You may not like the idea of following rules when trying to resolve a quarrel, but these rules will help you both resolve the issue instead of dancing around the topic or getting so angry that you just glaze over the whole thing.

Once you and your partner become accustomed to using active listening and the other tips listed above, your arguments probably will start to evolve into discussions intended to solve the problem instead of turning into heated arguments that do not solve anything. Active listening and the other techniques become habits when you use them frequently, and these techniques can take your long-distance relationship to the next level.

Tamsen's Tip

Active listening has to be something that the two of you agree to use. It will not work if only one of you is using this technique during a heated discussion.

Options for Long-Distance Communication

Not long ago, a long-distance relationship was doomed to only using telephone or mail for communication, and although these options were better than no communication, technology has blessed long-distance couples with the ability to stay in touch through a wide variety of methods. Depending on where you and your partner are, a long-distance relationship might not even seem that far removed from any other relationship, particularly if you are in the position to contact your partner any time, no matter where he or she is. Being able to see your partner — even if it is on a computer screen or using video chat on your phone — can make him or her seem not so far away.

Letters

Do not automatically dismiss the idea of writing letters to your partner while he or she is away from you. Although writing letters might seem like an old-fashioned method of communicating, many people feel it is a lost art that recipients still appreciate.

A letter says more than what is written on the page. A letter says, "I took the time to sit down and write this with my own hands because you are worth the time and effort it took to compose this letter." Receiving a letter in the mail — especially if it is unexpected — can be a real treat for your partner. Hand-written letters are not so common anymore, so this makes this method of communication all the more special.

If it has been a long time since you wrote a letter, rest assured that it is not a complicated process, and your partner is not expecting perfection (if he or she is even expecting a letter). If you have trouble thinking of things to write, try starting out with these ideas:

- Write a letter about how lucky you are to have your partner and why.

- Write about a special memory you have about the two of you, such as when you first met or when you first realized your partner was special.

- Write about something funny that happened in your day.

- Write about the dreams you have of what you will do the next time you are together or what the future holds for you both.

In a situation where your partner is temporarily away but will eventually return, consider including newspaper clippings or photos of things going on around town, so your partner can feel more connected to the community, despite being far away. This particularly is welcome if your partner is on a military deployment or somewhere different from what he or she is used to. If you have children together, be sure to include schoolwork or other pieces from the children. You might be surprised how much your partner will appreciate scribbles from the children, and this helps you stay connected as a family.

There are resources to help you with sending letters if you have a hard time composing something. Peruse the greeting card section the next time you are shopping to see what cards are available; you might be surprised by the vast variety of "Miss You" cards that do not need more than a signature and a stamp. If you are under the impression that all greeting cards are sappy, there is a chance you will encounter other types of cards, including funny card and cards that are romantic, but not in a sappy way.

Prefabricated greeting cards should augment your correspondence but not replace your correspondence altogether. Receiving a greeting card every week with nothing more than a quick signature from a partner might make the recipient feel like there is not enough effort being put into staying in touch. So, although there are ways to help you send notes to your partner through the mail, put effort into the process, and do not rely solely on greeting cards to convey your feelings to your partner.

Tamsen's Tip

Letters sent through the mail may seem outdated, but do not discount the power of an unexpected letter. If your partner is away, and you have children together, encourage your partner to write letters to the children on a regular basis. This can help the children feel connected in a way that sometimes email cannot accomplish.

Telephone

Hearing your partner's voice is important and special, even when the two of you cannot be in the same room. You are familiar with

your partner's unique speech patterns and can tell by the inflec-
tions in your partner's voice where the emphasis is on what your
partner is saying. When you are in a long-distance relationship,
your phone can be one of the most important tools you use to
stay connected.

There are practical considerations you and your partner should
keep in mind when using the telephone to keep in touch.

- Review your telephone service plan. It would be a rude
  surprise to receive a cell phone bill that is triple what

you are used to paying because you thought you had unlimited minutes but did not. If you know you are going to spend hours chatting with your partner, make sure your telephone service plan can support it.

- Set clear expectations with your partner for how often you will talk via telephone and at what times. This does not mean you cannot be spontaneous and call your partner unexpectedly to say you are thinking about him or her, but be realistic in your expectations. This means that if your partner is not allowed to use the phone while working, you will not leave 12 angry voice mails because your partner did not answer the phone at work. Be practical. Your partner is not at your beck and call, no matter how much in love the two of you are.

- Respect each other's preferences for talking on the phone. Maybe you only like to talk when there is a definitive topic at hand, but your partner can easily spend three hours on the phone talking about nothing in particular. The phone should be a tool to keep the two of you together and not a tool to distance you.

Do not allow these guidelines to stop you from having natural telephone conversations that occur organically. You do not want to be so focused on the practicality of phone conversations that you forget what a decent tool the phone is for staying connected. Your partner cannot be there for you all the time by phone, and you have to be all right with this.

You can use the phone to have a "date" with your partner when you watch a television show, prepare dinner, or even go to (separate) coffee shops together. These telephone dates are an excellent way to feel connected to your partner despite the distance. *In Chapter 7, you will learn more about having a phone date with your long-distance partner.*

If you are in a situation where telephone calls are rare (such as is the case with couples in vastly different time zones), the importance of coordinating a time for a phone conversation is increased. It can be frustrating to miss a call from your long-distance partner, but when you realize you have missed a call after not having spoken to your partner in a while and will not hear from your partner again for a while, this can shake you to the core. You might feel inadequate because you missed the call or allow your feelings to make you feel you have let your partner down by not sitting by the phone awaiting a call. If you accidentally miss a phone call from your partner — even if your partner rarely has access to a phone — do not allow yourself to dwell on it to the point where you feel horrible or inadequate as a partner. Feel guilt if you are intentionally avoiding phone calls from your partner, but not if you just miss a phone call.

Tamsen's Tip

When my husband was in Iraq, I would feel hugely guilty if I missed his call. I pictured him hopeful to get in touch with me and then disappointed when I did not answer the phone. I just had to accept that I cannot be available 24 hours a day and that I was doing the best I could.

When you are talking to your partner over the phone, listen to what he or she says and how he or she says it. It is one thing to say, "I miss you, too," but it is another thing when this is said distractedly or in a sarcastic tone. You do not have the benefit of seeing your partner's face during a phone conversation; so if you need clarification on something your partner has said, ask. It is better to make sure you understand what your partner is saying instead of walking away from the conversation more confused.

Texting

Texting is good for passing along chunks of information, such as, "Just thought you should know I am thinking about you" or "Please remember to pay the electric bill before Wednesday." Some long-distance couples enjoy having conversations via text because they are instantaneous and can be snuck in when a telephone conversation cannot. For example, a person riding the subway to work might not be comfortable with having a telephone conversation in public, but texting is a private situation and can happen while surrounded by people without sharing what is being said.

As with telephone conversations, there are practical considerations when texting with your long-distance partner.

- Not all cell phone providers automatically offer unlimited texts. Find out what your cell phone plan says about texts, and if you know you will be texting with your partner, figure out the best plan to make this an inexpensive option.

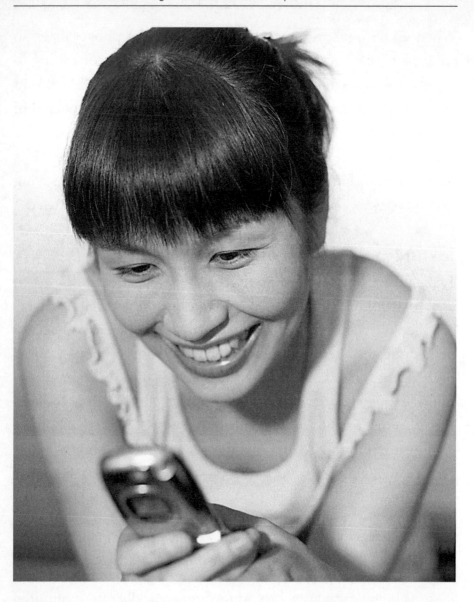

- Texts can be saved and shared with other people. You might be tempted to send suggestive texts (or photos in the form of a text, if your cell phone has the capability to do so), but keep in mind that once something is sent, there is no way of undoing it. Think about what would happen if you break up with your partner, your partner's friend borrows the cell phone to make a call and stumbles upon the suggestive text or photo, or you accidentally send the text to your boss. Think carefully before sending something via text that you would not want your grandmother to see.

- The way things are written sometimes does not effectively convey what it is you are trying to say. Even though texts are relatively quick methods of communication, reread — and maybe even speak aloud — what you have written to make sure there is nothing that could be misinterpreted.

Tamsen's Tip

Auto-correct, which is a cell phone's way of ensuring you spell everything correctly in the body of your text, can be just as annoying as it is convenient. If you are not careful, auto-correct might completely change the meaning of your text. My friend sent me a text inviting me to karaoke, and the next text said, "I want to cuddle with you." It turns out she was trying to say, "I want to sing with you," but the auto-correct stepped in when she misspelled the word "sing." We had a laugh about that one, but it was an excellent example of how texting can warp intended communication. For more examples, check out **http://damnyouautocorrect.com.**

Texting should not be a replacement for real conversation unless texting is your only option for staying in touch with your partner. Text conversations can get disjointed, and the brevity necessary for these conversations can halt progress if you are trying to have a serious conversation about your relationship or something else important. Consider texting to just be another communication tool, but not the preferred method of staying in touch.

You will learn about fighting fairly with your long-distance partner later in this chapter, but for now just remember that texting is not an effective method for having an argument with your partner. Texts are too abrupt and too restrictive to use for fighting, and it is generally inadvisable to use texts for having a heated discussion. If a text conversation seems to be evolving into an argument, agree to put the discussion on hold until you have the opportunity to speak about your differing points of view over the phone or in person, if possible.

Your partner has a life, too. If you send a text and do not receive an immediate response, this does not automatically mean you are being ignored. Your partner cannot always drop everything and respond to your text. If this is the case, do not allow yourself to be hurt or offended. It is one thing if your partner is truly ignoring you, but it is another thing if he or she is just busy.

Texting should be one of the several methods for communication you use to stay connected to your partner. Unless there is a particular reason why this is the only way the two of you can communicate, it should not be your main method.

Instant messaging

Instant messaging is a way to stay in touch with your long-distance partner. This method uses the computer to type messages to your partner and have a real-time conversation. Some instant messaging programs also allow you to send photos, videos, and links to websites in the conversation. *Look in the Appendix of this book for options for instant messaging programs.*

You and your partner will need an Internet connection to make instant messaging work. It helps if your Internet connection is fast because a slow connection can slow the conversation down. Some cell phones have the capability to support instant messaging, so this communication option is not limited to those people who can sit down in front of a computer.

Like texts, it is important to keep in mind that the things you send in an instant message conversation can be saved and shared. All it takes is for the other person to copy and paste the text of the conversation, and the entire chat can be sent to anyone else. There is also the possibility — however slim — that your partner might accidentally leave the instant message program up on his or her computer and someone else might come along and pose as your partner. Keep these things in mind for practical purposes when using instant messaging with your long-distance partner.

That being said, this can be an excellent tool for staying in contact with your partner. As long as you are both comfortable typing out the conversation, you can have long conversations when a telephone conversation might not be possible. Consider this option if your partner does not have ready access to a phone, if you worry about the telephone bill, or even if you want to sneak in a conversation while at work and trying to appear as if you are working on your computer. Keep in mind, however, that many employers monitor employees' computer activity, so you might not have any legal recourse if your boss is reading what you thought was a private instant message conversation with your partner.

If you have never tried instant messaging, do not allow the above warnings to dissuade you from trying it. Just be cautious about what you say in an instant message conversation. Your partner might not be the only person with access to what you say.

Some couples find that leaving an instant messaging program open on their computers allows spontaneous conversations to occur, which can be fun, as long as both people are available. If you and your partner plan to use instant messaging, be sure to update your status to reflect your availability to chat. For example, some instant messaging programs allow you to update your status as "Available to Chat," "Busy," or "Away." Keeping your status updated will let your partner know if you are truly available for a chat or if you are busy working and cannot stop what you are doing to have a conversation.

Instant messaging is a way to chat with your partner about your day. Although this should not be your preferred method to have serious discussions, it can be better to use instant messaging for serious discussions than texting if these are your only two options. The conversation can flow more smoothly with instant messaging, and it is easier to review what has already been said in the conversation.

CASE STUDY: INSTANT MESSAGING WHILE AWAY

Scott, a fan of instant messaging

Instant messaging drastically has improved my relationship while I am away from my wife. It is nice to have an avenue of communication that allows brief and easy conversations. This is especially handy when I am at work and cannot take a phone call or my wife is working on her computer. It is nice knowing I can talk with her just by opening up my laptop and connecting to the Internet.

I love using it because even though I am nine time zones ahead, we can meet and have a quick chat. One of the best features is how clear communication is versus talking on overseas phone lines. Phone calls can be difficult while working in an office with 13 other people trying to have their own phone conversations or deal with customers. Instant messaging also allows me to use emoticons to add expression that might be lost in an email or letter.

Using instant messaging can be frustrating in certain circumstances. The most common disruption to service is a result of an unstable Internet connection. Outside of losing my Internet service, my conversations are lost when the platform goes down. Either way, I have a limited window of time available to chat, and any interruption to service can be a bummer.

Email

Email is to society what written letters once were. There is a chance you are comfortable with how email works. The advantages to email is that it is delivered right away to your partner's inbox, and you can revise your draft several times before you send it to make sure you are getting your point across without any confusion.

Sending email once a day, if possible, can be nice. However, this depends on your preferences and capabilities. You might not have the time to send email every day, just as you might not enjoy the process of composing email and find a once-a-day email obligation to be daunting. A daily email can help because it is a predictable communication schedule and something that can be saved. When a partner is away from the person he or she loves, having a folder of email to read when he or she wants is a motivator and reminder of the love between both partners.

Some of the same rules for written letters apply for email. Reread what you write to make sure everything is clear, and there is no confusion as to what you are trying to say. Email is not the place for blatant accusations or angry diatribes. Fighting fairly will be discussed later in this chapter, but that email is one-sided. In a face-to-face conversation, both people can defend themselves if necessary. In an email format, if a long list of complaints is aired, this is more of a complaint letter than a correspondence between loving couples.

You might not have any other choice but to resort to email for your communication with your partner, depending on your situation. If this is the case, once the email is sent, there is no getting the email back. So, if you send a long, angry email to your partner accusing him or her of not being faithful (or whatever else is on your mind when you type the email), there no way to erase what you wrote after you sent the email, and your partner can keep the email. Heated conversations can fade in memory over time, but an angry email can be reread forever.

Video chat

One of the best technologies available for long-distance couples is video chat, which allows you to see your partner while talking to him or her. This is available over the Internet and with phones that have video chat capability. With video chat, you have the advantage of being able to see your partner during the conversation.

This erases the issue of not being able to see your partner's body language, which can help your communication immensely.

Not everyone is comfortable with video chat. For some, the thought of cameras trained on their faces makes them nervous and might compel them to act unnaturally. Video chat is not perfect; the quality of the video chat is largely dependent upon the Internet connection and the quality of the webcam used.

On the other hand, video chat is popular and widely available. Skype, which is one of the most popular methods for video chat available on the Internet, provides a simple setup process and is free to use.

Here are other interesting facts about Skype:

In 2010:

- Skype-to-Skype voice and video minutes totaled about 531 million minutes per day (194 billion minutes for the year).
- Skype-to-Skype and Skype to land lines/mobile voice and video minutes totaled about 207 billion minutes.
- Users sent more than 176 million SMS text messages through Skype.

At peak times, about 30 million concurrent users are logged into Skype at any given time (as of March 2011).

- Video Calling:
  - o In the first half of 2011, video calls accounted for about 43 percent of Skype-to-Skype minutes.
  - o At peak times, about half a million simultaneous video calls are made on Skype (as of June 2011).
  - o Peak video minutes occur on Sunday afternoons (GMT).
  - o On average, more than 4,000 hours of video is transmitted every minute on Skype (as of May 2011).
  - o About 75 percent of Skype's online users have made a video call.
  - o Skype users make an average of 300 million minutes of video calls per day (connected users as of June 2011).

Video chat can be helpful especially when you have children or pets because this can allow the partner who is away to see and interact with them. It helps to be able to see loved ones, even if it is not face-to-face. For someone who is perpetually away, video chat is the next best thing to being in the same room with a partner.

Although video chats do not result in transcripts of the conversation like texting, instant messaging, and emails can, most video chat programs have recording capabilities. Whether a screenshot (a frozen picture of a moment in the video chat) or a full recording of the entire conversation, keep in mind that your conversation might not remain private. Most employers reserve the right to monitor employee activities on company computers, and in certain instances, computer activity might be monitored for security reasons. Even if you completely trust your partner, computers are not infallible. A risqué video chat can wind up widely available if someone hacks into your computer or your partner's computer. So, although you do not have to censor yourself too much or present yourself as someone other than who you are while in a video chat, think twice before making the decision to pull off your shirt in front of the computer's camera.

If possible, schedule recurring video chats with your partner. This is dependent on whether you both enjoy the video chat process, and it might take time before video chatting becomes a smooth process for both of you. If both of you can fall into a pattern of having video chats once or twice a week, this can be an excellent method for you to connect with each other despite the miles. Some long-distance couples try to video chat at least once a day, and sometimes more than once a day.

Use video chat to include your partner in special events while he or she away. Set up a video chat for parties and other celebrations, so your partner can attend these functions virtually. This also can be a tool for having a long-distance date. *This will be discussed in more detail in Chapter 7.*

Work with What You Have

If you are in the enviable position of having access to the aforementioned communication tools, you have the ability to choose what works best for you and your partner. There is a chance you will settle on one main method of communication while augmenting it with the other forms available. The point is to stay in touch and stay connected. Long-distance relationships have a difficult time flourishing if the communication is not there.

CASE STUDY: EXPERT ADVICE

Dr. Joyce Morley,
AKA "Dr. Joyce, The Luv Doctor"

Communication in itself is a problem, but when people have long-distance relationships, it makes it even more difficult. Nonverbal behaviors are very important for communication, so it is a big problem not being able to see the nonverbals, not being able to see expressions, or to read each other. Communication is very important when you are talking about being in a relationship.

The other problem with communication in a long-distance relationship is not being able to touch each other. The couple is not having that physical intimacy — and not just sexually — that comes with being together. People have a thing called "skin hunger," which means they have a need to have someone to share laughter with and to touch and be close to. This can include a hug, a touch, or even a pat. There is just something different about being able to share a physical closeness. Telephone conversations can help, but it is not the same as being together. Skype can add some, but not as much as being in the same place at the same time.

The biggest issue with long-distance relationships is communication, but another thing to consider is trust, which goes hand in hand with communication. Trust issues can be at a heightened level with a long-distance relationship. Most people I work with who are in long-distance relationships have issues with trust. Can she trust him? Can he trust her? People who are insecure probably will find that their levels of insecurity are heightened when in a long-distance relationship.

If you do not trust someone, you are not going to communicate with him or her. If one person does not have that trust for the other, he or she is going to hold back on communication. It is an inhibitor and prohibits effective levels of communication.

People in long-distance relationships should try to get together as often as they can. The other important thing to communicate is having goals.

People stay in situations for the long term without having definitive goals as to when they are going to get together. They should ask each other, "When are we going to make a commitment to each other?" Someone at some point has to be able to say, "After six months or a year, am I willing to move here or there, and what are we going to do?" What compromises are they willing to make to be together? Because the relationship begins to wane, it begins to wear on them after awhile, and it makes it difficult emotionally.

Communication is especially important in relationships in which the two people have never met in person, such as when people meet online and live far away from each other. I am concerned about those types of situations, those people who have never met the other person but become exclusively involved. I think that we need to stop being so desperate to be in relationships with each other. We have to learn how to take our time, and we have to learn to find out more information. When I am speaking in front of a crowd, I tell them not only do you need to find out if your partner has a green card to make sure he or she is legally here. You also need to have a red, blue, and every color card you can think of to be able to understand the background as far as the family of origin is concerned. What are their relationships like with their families? Think about men with their mothers and women with their fathers. How do they communicate with each other?

You have to be able to meet in person. I do not put credence behind meeting someone online until you meet him or her in person. You can meet someone online, but it might not be the right time. You do not know the history of that person. Find out more information, and be serious about it.

Ask your partner, "How can we meet more?" Sometimes it means meeting halfway to save money. Think about birthdays, holidays, and making sure you can have these special times together. Always ask each other, "How can we bring this long-distance arrangement to a close as soon as possible?" It has to be a temporary thing. I have clients who have been in a long-distance relationship for a long time, and often, it does not work out. They just do not have any plans. They keep going and talking about it, but they do not work at it to come up with a solution.

Often, the problem is that someone does not want to commit. The person who does not want to commit is not comfortable where he or she is or is not willing to relinquish where he or she is. Sometimes he or she has other things going on; there could be another person in his or her life the person is not willing to give up or has something he or she is not willing to let go. A true long-distance relationship has to have an endpoint, and it has to be an endpoint both people agree on. They need to have written goals so they can look at those goals. There need to be dates they are working toward, and they should mark those dates on the calendar. We look at the plan that needs to be written, and we begin working toward what we have to do to make it happen. If I need to come there to look for jobs, or if you need to come here to look for jobs, what do we need to do? What are the actions? What are the expenses that are going to be there?

With open communication and trust come respect. Respect each other and each other's time, and evaluate your own issues of trust and insecurity. Do not play the blame game or allow name-calling, and as often as you can, talk to each other by phone. Email and texting can be cop-outs, and in many cases, I think it keeps people from having to communicate verbally. Make sure you are not disrespecting each other. There should be no hanging up the phone on each other. There should be a time for talking, but respect the lifestyle of the other person. Be responsible and accountable for your own behaviors and your own modes of communication.

Fighting Fairly

You are going to argue with your partner. Arguing is a staple of any relationship. Two people bring their own thoughts and feelings into the relationship, and it is unlikely that people will always agree about everything that comes up. Arguing is not unhealthy in a relationship, but much depends on how the fighting takes place. When an argument is resolved after both people have aired their feelings and a compromise results from the discussion, this serves to strengthen the relationship. It is when arguments become opportunities to try to hurt each other — or competitions to see who can be crowned "right" — that arguments take an ugly turn and wind up damaging the relationship.

There is a chance you have encountered arguments in a face-to-face setting, but the rules for fighting fairly change when you are in a long-distance relationship. This does not mean it is necessary

for you to hold in your feelings or just accept undeserved criticism from your long-distance partner. Instead, the point is to communicate your concerns effectively while also effectively listening to what your partner has to say.

Insecurities

Trying to trust someone you do not see on a regular basis can cause insecurities to grow. This can be a big problem with long-distance relationships, but as long as the two people involved acknowledge

insecurities and do not attempt to mask these feelings as something else, it does not have to mean the end to the relationship.

When insecurities are masked as something else, they might take the overt form of anger, jealousy, or even ambivalence. You feel insecure with your relationship because you know your partner works with a wide variety of people of the opposite sex and worry your partner will be attracted to someone else. Instead of voicing your insecurities in a reasonable way, such as, "I worry you will become attracted to someone you work with because you hardly get to see me," you might wrap your insecurities up in a blanket of other emotions, so you do not feel as vulnerable. An example of this is, "Why couldn't you answer your phone when I called? Were you too busy ogling your boss? You do not even care about me, do you?"

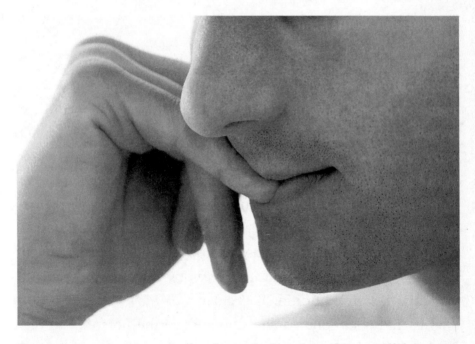

Say what you mean, and acknowledge that there will be times when you feel insecure in your long-distance relationship. There will be times when your partner cannot answer the phone or when an email is not responded to as quickly as usual. When these instances occur, insecurities might pile up and might even be the end of the relationship. Instead, acknowledge insecurities and discuss them with your partner. Wording is important here, especially when talking about issues involving trust. Instead of saying, "I have a hard time shaking the idea that you are cheating on me," which sounds like an accusation, try something along the lines of, "When you are away, my insecurities get the best of me, and I worry that you might stray," which puts the blame for the insecurities on you instead of your partner. Unless you have a valid reason for thinking your partner is gallivanting around town with someone else, avoid throwing the "cheating card" into a conversation when there is no real reason for it.

Be fair

When you acknowledge that there are bound to be insecurities in a long-distance relationship and that it is best to be honest and frank about your feelings instead of allowing your feelings to explode out in a twisted form, it becomes apparent that certain behaviors will do nothing but damage your relationship. For example, hanging up on your partner in a phone conversation can do even more harm in a long-distance relationship than it will in a traditional relationship. You might consider it the equivalent to walking away from a heated conversation, but when your primary method of communication is by telephone, it has the potential to cause additional problems or maybe even create a stigma that telephone conversations have the potential to turn sour. Telephone conversations that end abruptly in anger leave both partners feeling upset and perhaps even reluctant to pick up the phone again in the future. In this particular instance, it would be far better to tell your partner, "I am angry right now, so

I need to end this conversation, but I will call you after I have had a chance to cool down."

It might seem like the examples of things to say place the blame squarely on your shoulders, and this is true. Keep in mind that you are driven by your own emotions, and for that reason you have to take responsibility for them. You might think to yourself, "He makes me so mad," but it is more accurate to say, "I allow myself to get mad." Nobody can force you to feel a certain way; you have to take ownership of your responses. Instead of placing the blame on your partner for your emotions, be fair, and acknowledge that these are your emotions and that you are responsible for them.

Justified fighting

Arguments are going to happen, and sometimes these arguments are completely justified. If resolved to the satisfaction of both people, arguments actually can serve to strengthen a relationship. There can be something incredibly powerful about knowing that a disagreement can be faced head-on and eventually resolved; it lets both people in the relationship know that a simple argument is not going to be the end. When you are in a long-distance relationship, the stronger your bond is, the stronger your chance is of staying together despite the distance.

What happens if you or your partner does something that results in a big blow-up? When a huge, heated argument occurs — especially when it happens by phone or over the computer — it can be difficult to keep your emotions in proper perspective. Your mind might say, "I am frustrated, angry, and hurt," but your mouth might say, "You are the worst boyfriend/girlfriend ever, and I hate you." The nonverbal cues that might prompt you to react a certain way are absent, so, it might be even easier to allow your emotions to bubble over and explode. After all, there is a big difference between hearing your partner say, "I am sorry" over the phone or computer and seeing your partner say these words.

Here are tips for arguing fairly when in a long-distance relationship:

- Say what you mean. Your partner cannot read your mind, especially from miles away.

- Examine your emotions, and do not blame your partner for your own feelings.

- Do not allow your imagination to make the situation worse. Just because your partner does not answer the phone, it does not automatically mean your partner is involved in a torrid affair.

- Consider your partner's feelings. Hanging up on your partner or abruptly ending a computer conversation can intensify the damage.

- Keep in mind that the goal is not to avoid arguments entirely, but instead, it is to fight fairly and resolve issues in a way that will strengthen the relationship.

You will learn more about how to avoid sabotaging your relationship in the Chapter 9. Unfortunately, for many long-distance couples, they fall into the trap of sabotaging their relationships and wind up breaking up. You do not have to fall into this pattern. No matter what your specific situation, you can make your long-distance relationship work.

Chapter 4

The Masks People Wear

Who are you? This is a loaded question, but it is an important question to ask when dealing with any relationship, especially a long-distance relationship. Sometimes being in a relationship in which the majority of communication takes place over the phone or computer can make it too easy to present yourself as someone other than who you truly are. This can happen without you even realizing it. Think about which parts of you are exposed to your partner. Do you only share happy stories when chatting on the telephone, or do you omit problems when emailing your partner? By only presenting a perpetually happy version of yourself to your partner, you are putting on a happy mask that can cause big problems when the two of you are able to spend time together.

It can be difficult to be yourself when the majority of your communication with your partner is not face-to-face. When you are in a traditional relationship, your partner sees your impromptu emotional outbursts when something goes wrong, but in a long-distance relationship, you might censor these outbursts before contacting your partner. Although you certainly do not want to barrage your partner with everything that goes wrong throughout your day, you do not want to make everything seem so wonderful that when your partner gets the opportunity to spend time with you he or she is shocked by the difference in your demeanor or character. Here is an important piece of advice when in a long-distance relationship: Just be you.

Tamsen's Tip

I lost one of my main writing jobs weeks after my husband left for a deployment to Afghanistan. I figured he had enough stress, and I did not want to burden him with more problems, so I did not bring it up when we talked. My friend Dave, who is frequently deployed, too, urged me against keeping this from my husband. "You have to share it all with him," he said. "It does not matter if it is good or bad; sharing it with him helps him feel connected while he is gone." Dave was right. I asked my husband if he wanted to hear the bad stuff, and he emphatically assured me that sharing everything with him — good or bad — helps him feel closer to home. I also felt better because I did not feel like I was keeping something important from him.

Why People Wear Masks

A long-distance relationship can start to feel like a game after a while. This happens because of the distance; you have your "normal" life, which includes your work, friends, and immediate surroundings. Then, on the other hand, you have a partner who is not part of your "normal" life because he or she is not around. Your partner might only appear in your life periodically, and when your partner shows up on your doorstep, it is interrupts the normal flow of life you have. Even if you are elated to see your partner, it is a deviation from your typical routine.

Wearing a mask is a defense mechanism. Being in a long-distance relationship can be painful. You want to be able to hug your partner at the end of the day. You long to share everyday experiences with your partner. If you have children with your partner, you might feel resentment that your children are deprived of daily interactions with your partner. Many emotions can be present in a long-distance relationship; so emotional coping tools can pop up.

This does not mean that wearing a mask and presenting yourself as something other than who you are is healthy. To the contrary, this can be damaging to your relationship and can leave you feeling as though you are going through life playing too many roles. You will wind up feeling exhausted and wondering who you are. Although you might form these masks as simple coping mechanisms — and perhaps not even realize that you are doing so — your partner might regard it as deceptive. How would you feel if your partner was always sunny and positive when talking to you on the phone but completely melancholy the moment you were together in the same room?

The Split Personalities

The masks people create when they are in long-distance relationships are not the same as "split personalities" that are characteristic of Dissociative Identity Disorder, formerly known as "Multiple Personality Disorder." So, if you have found you have masks of your own, do not assume this means you need to rush off to a therapist for psychoanalysis. Just recognize that you have formed these masks, and you need to make an effort to present yourself as you truly are to your partner.

Who are you?

You cannot expect your partner to know who you are if you are not even sure who you are. With a partner away, you may have ample time for self-reflection that will allow you to search your own feelings and desires and figure out who you are. Think about it this way: Are you who you want to be, or are you who you think people expect you to be?

If you and your partner have a solid relationship, there is a good chance that your partner still enjoys being with you even when you do not feel particularly cheerful, social, or even polite. This is not to say that your partner happily should accept you berating him or her or stomping around the house in a huff because your coffee did not turn out exactly as you want it made. Instead, it means that even on days when you cannot muster the energy to handle everything you usually handle, your partner is still just as enamored with you as those days when you are on your "A-game." Partners in a flourishing long-distance relationship accept each other for who they really are, and they do not try to put on a show in an attempt to present a perfect image to one another.

Be you. The truth is that if you do not know who you are, then there is little chance of your long-distance relationship flourishing because you may not be presenting yourself to your partner in an authentic way. Figure out what you want your life to be, and not necessarily what your family or friends want your life to be. When you have figured this out, you then need to decide how your partner fits into the grand scheme of things when it comes to your authentic life. Remember: Exploring self-realization and "finding yourself" does not automatically mean your relationship is doomed. You might both find that your relationship is strengthened by exploring who you truly want to be.

You with your partner

Do you change when you are with your partner? Whether you feel more at ease than usual or if you are exhausted from desperately trying to be perfect during the limited time you have together, you might feel as though you are not yourself when you spend time together. Although initial awkwardness is common and expected among long-distance couples when they are able to have time together, if you spend that time feeling as though you are putting on an act, then you have fallen into an unhealthy pattern of trying to be someone you are not. This is not good for you, your partner, or your relationship. *You will learn more about making the most of the time you have together in Chapter 8.*

People who are in long-distance relationships might feel pressure to present a perfect version of themselves during visits. Spending time with your partner face-to-face can be a rare treat for people in long-distance relationships, so it is easy to see how time together might be something you desperately want to go well. You might fear that a bad visit might be the end of the relationship; after all, it can be hard work to make a long-distance relationship flourish, and face-to-face visits can be seen as the reward for all the hard work. If you do not fashion what you think is a perfect visit, then you might worry that your partner will no longer want to put forth the effort to keep the two of you together.

However, there is no such thing as perfection in a relationship. There are going to be times when you are cranky, irritated, tired, sick, or just plain boring, and the same goes for your partner. People in traditional relationships deal with these things all the time because they are around their partners more frequently than those people in long-distance relationships. Everyone gets moody sometimes, and just because your partner is away does not mean you have to mask these emotions. Honesty is the best policy. After all, if your partner was grouchy after a rough day at work, would you rather he or she told you up front that the grouchiness was a direct result of a tough day or have him or her pretend everything was fine when it was not?

When you have the opportunity to be with your partner face-to-face, be yourself. This does not mean to spend all your time together complaining about everything, but do not try to hide who you are. If your relationship has any hopes of flourishing and overcoming the inevitable issues that come with long distance, make sure you are not putting on masks and pretending to be something you are not. If your partner truly cares about you, there should be no need for you to pretend. Give your partner the opportunity to fall in love with the real you.

You apart from your partner

It is quite typical to feel you are one person when you are with your partner and then feel different when chatting over the phone or on a computer. These varying forms of communication are so different it might prompt you to vary how you present yourself

depending on which form of communication you are using at the time. Talking on the phone or chatting online is different from having a discussion in the same room.

Some people fall into a rut of presenting a different version of themselves in these conversations, particularly when it comes to avoiding any topics of possible conflict.

Think about how easy it is to realize that something is troubling your partner when you are having a conversation face-to-face. Your partner might look away instead of looking you in the eye or might fidget his or her hands. On the other hand, when a conversation takes place over the phone or the computer, it is easier to mask tension.

It is normal to feel disconnected from your spouse when you are unable to have any time together. As a result, you might find yourself putting on an act when you do get the chance to chat with your partner, and you might not even realize you are doing it. In stressful situations, such as a military deployment, there is a strong desire to ensure all conversations are pleasant.

Phone and Internet conversations can enable people to cover up things that might otherwise be revealed. Masks are not necessarily unintentional. In instances when one partner is cheating on another, it can be harder to discover the issue when the main form of communication is not face-to-face. In this instance, the mask the cheating partner wears is intentional and fundamentally damaging to the relationship.

You with other people

Having a strong social circle can be of tremendous value when your partner is not around because you do not feel as isolated as you would if your life lacked social interaction. Problems can arise, however, when you are one person with your friends and another person with your partner. In this instance, you have the potential to harm not only your romantic relationship, but also the relationships you have with your friends.

If you have the tendency to be one way with your friends and another way with your partner, do not be shocked when your friends react oddly at how you behave when your partner visits. You might be accused of acting like someone else or playing the part of a perfect partner. This situation will not help endear your partner to your friends because they might assume it is your partner compelling you to act oddly. In this instance, you are setting up a metaphorical time bomb among your social circle; it will only be a matter of time before someone pulls you aside and asks about your differing behavior.

There are those friends who bring out the goofy side of you, and there are those friends who are introspective, so you take a calmer stance with them. It is natural (and normal) to adjust slightly to each person you interact with, but it becomes a different matter when your personality does a major shift when it comes to your group of friends versus your partner. It is an easy pattern to fall into; you might see your friends often, but do not get to see your partner as much. The trick is to try to present who you really are to your friends and your partner.

Avoiding Masks

It is difficult to wind up wearing masks if you are true to yourself consistently, but it can still occur. When you are in a romantic relationship, and you do not spend much time with your partner, you might find that your relationship progress has the tendency to stagnate if you do not make a concerted effort to move it forward. You might have an unconscious or even conscious desire to make sure your partner does not feel as though everything is changing while he or she is gone, so, if you stay exactly the same, then there will not be any problems.

This idea does not work because you are not a static being. You are constantly changing and evolving your identity, and your surroundings change as well. Suppose the next time you will see your partner is in six months, and then, think about all the changes that can occur in your life in half a year. What are the chances you will be exactly the same person you were when your partner left six months ago? You are bound to change, and there is no reason to mask these changes.

Once again, this is where communication is important in a long-distance relationship. You will find yourself wearing a mask with your partner if you censor yourself and do not share the changes going on in your life. Suppose you go back to college, join a church, or jump feet-first into your dream of quitting your job and writing that novel while your partner is away? These things

change people, and although the changes might be incredibly positive, big events in your life will change who you are and how you spend your days. These are the changes to convey to your partner; otherwise, your partner might feel left out and might panic because of all the changes he or she is missing or does not understand.

CASE STUDY:
EXPERT ADVICE

Reverend Darrin Kimpson

If a long-distance couple came to me and said they felt disconnected because of the miles apart, I would say consistent calling and using the benefit of technology to see each other visually is important. Bring in the spiritual, and have God be the one who keeps you connected by doing devotions together and praying with each other; those are what can help you be connected.

I would suggest to them first to have a frank discussion about their spiritual beliefs to figure out where they both stand. If a couple does not have much interest spiritually, it can be a growing thing together.

Having coexisting spiritual beliefs in a relationship can help strengthen the connection while apart. If there is an openness you both have, try to include God in this journey. Take advantage of the openness you have talking about that with each other when you have a chance to talk. If there is something that keeps people connected or gets them connected in the first place, it would be things of substance.

Just talking about the weather does not keep us connected in depth, but if you talk about real-life, deep things, you could consider talking about what you think about God and his or her role in keeping the two of you strong while you are away from each other. Even if you have not talked about it, this is an opportunity to grow closer to each other and stay connected because you are talking about deep stuff. Open up conversations with, "What do you think about God?" or "Do you think God has a role in bringing us together?" If you do not come to the same conclusions right away, it is all right. Talks like this do not mean you suddenly have to proclaim you are going to start going being more spiritual. But if you choose to start exploring it, I think God could use the openness to do work.

It could lead to simple prayers, with you and your partner praying together or one person praying and the other person listening. Even if it turns out you start talking about spiritual things and God and that does not turn out to be something you do consistently, figure out the things that are distracting you. Find out what things exist that perhaps draw you away from your partner. Are there things or people you are spending too much time with that are causing you to drift? Whether someone is spiritual or not, he or she should ask himself or herself, "Are there things that I am too involved with or a person I am too involved with that makes it to where I am not missing you anymore?" I would not say that people should not keep themselves busy or that people should make themselves miss their partner, but are you keeping yourself so busy that it is causing a disconnect?

I know about long-distance relationships not only as a pastor who counsels couples, but also because I participated in a long-distance relationship when I was younger. It did not end well. I dated a girl in high school for about nine months, and then she went away to college. She was a year older than me, so I was still in high school. Gradually, throughout the fall of my senior year, I started to sense a little bit of a change in her behavior, and she became a little more distant. I also noticed that, for some reason, she was not very motivated to come back home often to see me.

At that point in my life, I was so into her that she could treat me like dirt, and I did not even see it. I thought she was the one, but then I had a few of my friends tell me she was cheating on me. They knew from their friends and from their older sisters who were the same age as my girlfriend that she had been seen with other guys at her college campus. My initial reaction was disbelief because I thought she would have told me. I finally asked her; it had come to the point where she was purposely treating me like dirt because she did not have the nerve to say, "Yes, I am now dating someone else." She found a guy a couple of years older than me at college.

I am not a fan of long-distance relationships because of that. She went away, and the distance caused her to be influenced by her new environment. We quickly drifted apart. Overall, I do not think we had the maturity at that age to handle the distance.

Shed Awkwardness

If you initially met your partner face-to-face, having a long-distance relationship that consists largely of telephone and computer communication can feel awkward and forced. This is especially true if you do not care for these forms of communication, which is the case with many people. It is one thing to use the phone to order a pizza or to compose email intended for business correspondence, but it is another thing to try to convey your emotions using these methods.

Here are tips for making the most of the communication methods available to you:

- Picture your partner in front of you when you have a phone conversation. If it helps, look at a photo of your partner during the conversation, or close your eyes to block out everything else around you.

- Download Skype, and try to use this form of communication frequently. This allows you to see your partner while you chat, which removes some of the communication barriers that can come with long-distance relationships. If you feel awkward in front of the camera or distracted by your own face in the computer screen, turn off the feature that allows you to see yourself on the screen and just concentrate on the image of your partner.

- Compose email as though you are having a conversation with your partner. Avoid making the email sound like business or academic correspondence, which initially might be difficult for you if you spend time writing formal correspondence for work or school. Sometimes it helps to read email aloud before sending it; if it sounds forced or stuffy to you, there is a chance it will sound forced or stuffy to your partner.

- Tell your partner you feel awkward. Your partner would rather have you admit that you feel awkward chatting on the phone or over the Internet instead of you sounding uncomfortable but not explaining why.

- Accept that the forms of communication available to you might not be ideal, but they are certainly better than nothing. It was not long ago when couples had to rely solely on postal mail when away from each other. Now is a convenient time to be in a long-distance relationship because the opportunities for staying in touch are numerous.

- Give yourself time to adjust. Even if you are not a big fan of talking over the phone, you might be pleasantly surprised eventually to find that you do not mind it, particularly when talking over the phone gives you the opportunity to chat with your partner.

When you feel awkward about talking on the phone or over the Internet, make sure not to put up a mask. You might choose your words too carefully, or you might not delve as deeply into the conversation as your partner would like. Do not allow your dislike for these forms of communication to stifle your personality or thoughts. If you want your relationship to thrive and flourish, you have to become accustomed to using whatever forms of communication are available to you and your partner.

Chapter 5

Setting Goals

S etting goals is an important step to take in a long-distance relationship. Most people consider a long-distance arrangement a temporary one, with an eventual goal of being physically together at some point. If no definitive goals are set for the relationship, how can you know if you are heading in the right direction? If you and your partner work together to define what you want in your relationship, then you can take proper steps to move the relationship toward your eventual goal.

When you are both in agreement about short-term and long-term goals, certain decisions become easier to make as a couple. When questions arise regarding topics such as job offers, it is important to ask, "How can we best solve this issue while still working toward our goals?" Setting goals can be a daunting task, especially if you are cautious about confronting your partner with a request for clarification on your relationship status. When it comes down to it, though, the point is to flourish in your long-distance relationship. Without clearly defined goals, it is difficult to flourish because you do not know what you are aiming for.

The Importance of Goals

Do not discount the importance of looking toward the future in your long-distance relationship. Although some couples try to avoid having a big talk about the future, when you are not physically near your partner, it becomes even more important to define clearly where you expect your relationship to wind up. So, although you initially might feel uncomfortable bringing up the big question of where the relationship is going, the question might help to solidify your relationship and allow it to flourish as you work toward your mutual goals.

Although important, you do not want to focus merely on your long-term goals. Short-term goals also need to be addressed. When is the next time the two of you will be together in the same room? How often do you want to have telephone conversations? How many texts per day do you need from your partner to feel you are getting the right of amount of attention?

Discussing your mutual goals means there are no big question marks in your relationship. If you know the two of you have the eventual goal of someday living together, the mutual decisions you make can lead toward that goal. If you know your partner expects you to call every night before going to bed, you will understand when your partner is sad when you forget to call. Your relationship goals clearly define your short-term and long-term directions, and when your relationship's direction is defined, it becomes easier to navigate.

The eventual goal of being together and someday shedding the label of "long-distance relationship" is one of the most important decisions you can make together. Though it is entirely possible to flourish in your long-distance relationship for an extended time, there is a chance that you want the opportunity to grow old together someday. If your partner is truly the person you want to spend the rest of your life with (or if you and your partner have already made this decision, and circumstances have kept you physically apart), then one of your biggest and most important goals will be to be together eventually and no longer do long distance. Without this goal, you and your partner will be left to wonder whether the long-distance arrangement is worth it.

Calm down

If reading about the vast importance of defining your relationship goals makes you feel anxious, take a deep breath, and realize that this is not something you have to do this minute. Your partner will be quite confused if you suddenly call him or her and demand to know where the relationship is going and when exactly the two of you can live in the same town. If your partner does not realize your sudden interrogation is coming from a desire to make your relationship flourish, he or she might feel suffocated and, perhaps, even panic.

Before talking to your partner about setting goals for your long-distance relationship, take a moment to pause, and ask yourself this question: What do you want? Do you like things the way they are, or are there changes you would like to see in your relationship? Do you have a deep desire someday to live with your partner, or does the thought of giving up the freedom your long-distance arrangement allows make you feel nervous? It is important to know what you want before you start asking your partner what he or she wants, otherwise you will not know if the two of you are in sync and moving toward the same goals.

Put simply; be prepared to know what you want in your relationship before you ask the same question to your partner. You do not have to have an answer carved in stone, but have an idea of what you want to hear from your partner before you even ask.

Tamsen's Tip

Do not feel selfish in examining what you want out of your relationship. You are entitled to know what you want and to make your desires clearly known to your partner. You will have a difficult time being on the same page as your partner if you do not accurately convey your ideas of what the relationship should look like now and down the road. Your partner cannot read your mind.

How to Set Goals

Setting goals does not have to be a huge endeavor. Think about the goals you set throughout your day already. You might have a goal of what time you will eat your lunch, what you will eat, and what time you will get back to whatever it was you were doing before you stopped to eat lunch. When you realize you set goals on a continual basis, the idea of setting goals for your long-distance relationship might not seem as daunting.

Keep in mind that these are not goals to set on your own, nor are they goals to keep to yourself. Although where you eat lunch does not affect your long-distance relationship, it certainly affects your relationship when you decide to make a goal of visiting your partner at least once a month. What if it is not feasible for your partner to visit you every month? There might be financial constraints or schedule problems that make it impossible to meet the goal of monthly visits. If you set this goal in your mind, yet neglect to pass this expectation along to your partner, your relationship might encounter difficulties when you find your goal is not working. This is an instance where goal setting should have been partnered with open communication to avoid frustration for everyone involved.

To get started in setting goals, here are questions to consider:

- Where do you expect your relationship to go?

- Where do you think your partner expects your relationship to go?

- What would be the ideal situation for your relationship in a few months? A year from now? Five years from now?

- What changes need to be made before you can accomplish your goals?

You already might have covered these questions with your partner. Perhaps you already are engaged or married, and the long-distance arrangement is a temporary one, so you know your goal of being back together under the same roof is an eventual goal you will meet. It is still a good idea to explore the other possible goals the two of you might have, while also discussing personal goals that might only initially pertain to one of you but eventually will affect you both. For example, suppose you always have assumed you eventually would return to graduate school and are just waiting until the time is right. This goal should be discussed with your partner, especially if the two of you have never discussed it before. What if your partner has no idea your plan is eventually to return to school and has the same plan in mind? At some point, the two of you will find yourselves in a situation in which both of you want to return to school, but if there is not enough money or time, someone is going to have to compromise. It is better to have this conversation earlier as opposed to later.

Here are tips to help you determine your goals, as an individual and as a couple:

- Examine your personal goals and the goals you have for your relationship, and consider your partner's goals .

- Think about long-term and short-term goals, and eliminate any that are not feasible.

- Compose a list of the goals that are directly or indirectly related to your long-distance relationship's success.

- Once you both agree that your goals are important, you now have a tangible list of goals that will help guide future decisions about your relationship.

Keep in mind that goals certainly can change. You do not want to fall into the trap of thinking your list of goals is the be-all and end-all guideline for every decision you make as a couple. Instead, consider the list of goals to be what is right for you now, and agree that a time might come when you will have to be flexible about where your relationship is heading. After all, you do not want to pass up an extraordinary career opportunity or not get to purchase your dream home at a reduced cost just because these unexpected opportunities were not listed on your goal list. Take life as it comes, and use your goal list as a guide, but with the understanding that goals can change frequently. The important thing is to agree mutually on your relationship goals.

CASE STUDY: ONE GOAL AT A TIME

Kyung, met his true love in the unlikeliest of places

We met shortly after I arrived in Kandahar in July 2007 for my second military deployment to Afghanistan. I was surprised to find a Korean snack bar on the base. A woman arrived about two weeks after I arrived to manage the snack bar. She was Korean, and so am I, and we used to joke that we were probably the only two Koreans on the entire base. We immediately struck up a friendship, and throughout the next few months, we got to know each other better. It quickly became apparent that we had much in common. We were the same age, as were our sisters and our mothers. She even had an aunt who lived in Los Angeles, which is where I am originally from.

We would often talk into the wee hours of the morning at the only 24-hour coffee joint on base. We would talk about everything. Our friendship grew into what eventually developed into a huge crush on my part. When it came time for me to head home in January, I mustered up enough courage to confess my true feelings for her. I must admit that I had no idea how it would even work for us to stay together if she accepted my heart, but I was incredibly happy when she admitted she had feelings for me, too.

We parted ways and decided to take it one day at a time. We remained committed to getting to know each other better. It was not easy. In the months after my departure, she was still in Afghanistan. The Internet was not nearly as readily available then, so I routinely racked up several hundred dollars worth of phone bills calling her cell phone.

Fast forward to the following summer of 2008. We found ourselves in familiar surroundings once again; I had moved closer to home to Los Angeles, and she had moved back to Guatemala where she had lived and worked before she went to Afghanistan. In July, I made the first of my four trips to Guatemala that year. Each time we saw each other, our feelings for each other grew stronger. Then, in October of that year, I proposed to her in Guatemala.

The rest, as they say, is history. We are now married and blessed with a beautiful baby boy. We found out about the pregnancy three days before I departed for a deployment to Iraq.

It goes without saying that communication was the absolute key in making our long-distance relationship work. I think what was also important in our case, aside from sharing the same cultural background and values, was that we knew being together would make each other better. We shared the common denominator of both coming from broken homes, and we were committed to not repeating the same mistakes our parents made. Early in our relationship, we set the goal of creating a household filled with love and laughter. When you share a mutual commitment, and when you honor the promises you have made to each other, it certainly makes the journey more worthwhile and serves to strengthen the relationship's bond.

Putting Plans in Motion

You have your list of goals for the long term and the short term. Now an important step for putting your plans into motion is figuring out how to concentrate on your goals. As was the case with composing your original list, this is not something to do on your own and then expect your partner to come along for the ride.

Concentrating on your goals is something that should be done together, and each goal should get the seal of approval from both people involved.

Figure out which goals are most important to you and to your partner while also examining which goals will best serve to strengthen your relationship. For example, if you both agree that having monthly visits with each other is more important than saving up for a large expense, such as buying a home together or having an elaborate wedding, then the goal of monthly visits will be more important than your long-term goal with a major expense. It will become apparent as you find that many of your goals are related in one way or another; at the least, you will find you have to wait on some of your goals to make the other goals happen.

Try to be realistic when prioritizing your goals. Look at the possible repercussions associated with your goals, especially emotional and financial. A goal of visiting your partner each month might be incredibly beneficial to your emotional connection, but the financial impact might be too much for your checkbook to handle. So, although it is good to see each other once a month to feel emotionally connected, your relationship might start to suffer when you find that the frequent travel expenses are too expensive. Being in love is good, but being overdrawn on your bank account and delinquent on your credit card bill is enough to put a damper on any relationship. Do not allow romance to override practicality because this, inevitably, will lead to a relationship you cannot maintain.

When priorities differ

You might find that your priorities are different from those of your partner, and with some couples, this can be a problem. Suppose you and your partner spend time composing lists of long-term goals and then comparing them over the phone only to find that your No. 1 goal of having a baby differs from your partner's of traveling the world. When you discover the two of you do not necessarily have the same goals to work toward, this can be a jarring revelation.

You already know that communication in a long-distance relationship is of the utmost importance. If you discover you and your partner have vastly different goals, take this as an opportunity to discuss what your goals should be together, and do not automatically assume your differing goals are a solid indication that your relationship is doomed. If the two of you can talk about your main priorities openly without allowing the discussion to turn into an argument, you might find that your goals can work quite well together. Maybe "traveling the globe" was not on your goal list because it did not seem like a feasible goal, but once you talked it through with your partner, you realized it might be something you could accomplish together. Perhaps your partner did not put much thought into having children but after discussing it, decided a baby is in the cards down the road. Having mutual goals that have been discussed thoroughly can make for a solid foundation for a couple, particularly when they are in a long-distance relationship. When you have solid goals you are both working toward, you still connected despite being physically apart. This can strengthen your relationship.

Tamsen's Tip

Red flags should go off in your head if your long-term, long-distance partner refuses to discuss setting plans in motion so the two of you can live closer to one another, especially if you and your partner see each other infrequently. Some people cling to a long-distance relationship because they do not want to make a commitment. If you find yourself in this situation, examine whether this relationship actually has the chance to flourish or if your partner is set on keeping the relationship stagnant forever.

Not all differing goals can be melded together so cohesively. Take the same example of the couple with one partner who wants to have a baby and the other partner who wants to travel the world. What happens when the travel-loving partner makes the proclamation that he or she does not want a baby now and will never want to have a baby? If you are the partner who has envisioned eventually having a family, finding out your partner will never want to have children will force you to take a hard look at your relationship and where it is going. Can you give up the dream of having children? Do you think your partner eventually will reconsider? Should you leave your partner and try to find someone who has the same goals as you? *You will learn more about deciding to call it quits in Chapter 10.* However, for now, do not assume that differing goals mean the relationship must come to a screeching halt.

Your goal list is more of an outline than a solidified schedule for how the future of your relationship will go. Just because your partner does not list the same goals as you now does not mean they will not appear on the list in the future. Use the tools for communication you have to openly express how you feel about the differences on your lists of goals. If you allow your mind to make illogical, cognitive leaps, such as "He did not list having a baby on his list. He must not want to have a baby with me. He thinks I am inadequate and unfit to be the mother to his child. This relationship is doomed," then your relationship certainly will suffer. Instead, be truthful and open with your partner about your concerns. Tell your partner you are surprised to not see a baby (or whatever your goal is) on his or her list, share that this goal is at the top of your list, and invite an honest discussion about the differences between the lists. Do not hurl accusations or be hurt by anything that appears on your partner's list, and listen carefully to what your partner has to say about his or her goals. One of the worst things you can do is to not listen and instead, formulate your rebuttal in your head while waiting for your turn to talk. This will not result in a productive discussion.

You might not be able to have this discussion with your partner face-to-face, but the same rules apply. Keep in mind what you have learned about telephone and email communications, and when you need clarification about something, ask for it instead of just assuming that you understand the intended meaning to be something insulting. If you are in a situation in which the distance between the two of you forces this conversation to take place over time — such as would be the case if the discussion had to take place through postal mail or through a series of emails — be patient. When an important discussion about your goals has to take place and when there are differences that must be discussed, it can be incredibly difficult to be long distance because it hampers the speed and effectiveness of communication.

You are talking about short-term and long-term goals, and when it comes down to it, there is no rush to get everything solved right this moment. Give it time.

Understanding Exclusivity

You might be wondering why a discussion about exclusivity is in a chapter about setting relationship goals. The answer is simple: Your list of shared goals will fall under the assumed umbrella of exclusivity to each other, and if both partners are not on board with being exclusive, the rest of the goals might fall apart.

If you are in a long-distance relationship where exclusivity has not been discussed or even assumed, then you might want to put the brakes on any discussion about your mutual goals until the two of you can figure out the status of your relationship. Do you want to discuss traveling the globe or having babies with someone who is still dating other people?

For your long-distance relationship to flourish, the two of you might want to be exclusive with each other. Being in a long-distance relationship can be difficult, but it is worth it if you know there is the potential for a future between the two of you. Putting effort into a relationship when you do not even know if your partner is fully on board with being your partner is not much of a relationship. If you are going to take the plunge and say the two of you are involved in a long-distance relationship — and you both want the relationship to flourish — it should be stated clearly that this relationship is exclusive and that you are committed to each other. This means no dates with other people and no on-line flirtations with other people, and there should be a shared list of goals between the two of you about where your relationship eventually will go.

This can be a tricky discussion if it has not yet occurred naturally. The truth is that if you have not heard the words from your partner that the two of you are exclusive with each other, you might find that your partner does not realize the two of you are not supposed to date other people. It might seem like a cop-out when your partner thinks, "How was I supposed to know that I am not allowed to see other people?" But this is how some minds work. For some people, exclusivity has to be spelled out. Decide what exclusivity means to you, find out what it means to your partner, and make sure you are on the same page. For you, exclusivity might allow you to go out with people of the opposite gender as long as you do not get intimate with them, but to your partner, exclusivity might mean you do not even have lunch with anyone of the opposite gender. It is not enough to say, "We are exclusive" in a long-distance relationship. The two of you should be able to say, "We are exclusive, and this is what being exclusive means to us."

Exclusivity is one of the most important decisions the two of you can make when trying to make your long-distance relationship flourish. If you are going to put this much effort into a relationship, the payoff should be that you know your partner is putting at least as much effort into the relationship as you are. If you do not have an exclusive relationship, it becomes too easy to stray and lose sight of your mutual goals as a couple. If you want your relationship to thrive, exclusivity is a decision that has to be made together.

Avoid the Cheating Trap

When you are in a long-distance relationship, the threat of one of you straying from the relationship is real and potentially heightened by the fact that the two of you cannot monitor each other's activities like you could if you lived under the same roof. This is certainly not to say that everyone is just waiting for the opportunity to cheat on his or her partner; most people do not set out to have an affair. For many people who wind up cheating, it starts out innocently but then turns into something else entirely.

You and your partner need to be clear about the expectations you set for each other when it comes to other people. You cannot blow up at your partner for having lunch with a coworker of the opposite sex if the two of you have not clearly stated that one-on-one lunches with people of the opposite sex are off limits. Talk to each other about expectations and perceptions. Your partner might not think he or she is doing anything wrong when going over to a friend's house for a movie night, but when that friend is of the opposite sex and the movie night goes late into the evening with no one else present, your perception of the situation might be different than the perception of your partner. You see it as an opportunity for your partner's friend to make a move while your partner sees it as an opportunity to see a movie with a friend.

If you and your partner have clear expectations set for each other about interactions with people of the opposite sex, it becomes difficult to argue about what is "right" and what is "wrong." Instead, you rely on what your partner has told you about his or her comfort level with what you do, and in turn, you have revealed what you find acceptable. If you have not yet had this discussion with your partner, start with these questions:

- What is unacceptable behavior with someone of the opposite sex?

- Are one-on-one interactions with people of the opposite sex acceptable? Does this change if it is related to work?

- Is it all right to text friends of the opposite sex?

- Is it all right to sleep over at a friend's house?

- Is going out drinking with a group of people acceptable?

There are no right or wrong answers to these questions. The "right" answer to these and related questions are the answers that you and your partner agree on. It is incredibly important to set guidelines with your partner when you are away from each other; this is not an area you want to remain vague on your mutual expectations for behavior. You might assume that your partner has the same expectations as you on this topic, but unless the two of you talk it through, you might be surprised to find your partner has been engaging in activities that you find unacceptable even if they are not classified as "cheating." How would you feel if your partner spent the night in the same bed as a friend of the opposite sex but then rationalized it by saying there was a storm and he or she did not want to drive home? Your partner might see this as nothing more than accepting a friend's generous offer of a place to stay on a stormy night, but you might see it as grounds for breaking up. Perception should be a huge part of figuring out what is acceptable for you and for your partner.

You cannot control what your partner does while away from you, but you can take responsibility for your own actions and not fall into the cheating trap. Even if you do not realize it, someone might view your long-distance situation as an oppor-tunity to swoop in and give you the emotional and physical attention you cannot get from your partner. You might appear to be needy or vulnerable, and this can be the case even if you do not portray neediness or vulnerability; it is enough that your partner is miles away.

Beware of friends of the opposite sex who appear eager to be your sounding board, or worse yet, who say things along the lines of, "If your partner loved you, he/she would be here right now" or "What your partner does not know will not harm him/her." Be on the lookout for people who seem excessively affectionate. It is one thing for a genuine friend to give you a big hug, but it is another thing entirely for a friend to start rubbing your back sen-suously or hold a hug for longer than what would be considered reasonable among friends. Listen to the voice inside your head; if your internal voice starts saying your friend is making a move on you, there is a chance you are right.

Continuing to play the flirting game with someone who is at-tracted to you is extremely risky. It might feel incredible to have someone pay attention to you and make you feel appreciated, but when it comes down to it, you have to decide if you want to be committed to your partner or if you want something else. Trust cannot be overemphasized as one of the most important factors in a successful long-distance relationship, and if you are doing things that betray your partner's trust — whether he or she finds out or not — it is completely damaging to your relationship.

Surround yourself with people who care about you, but remove yourself from the presence of people who want more from you. If you get the feeling one of your friends might have feelings for you beyond friendship, use caution, and do not allow yourself to get into a situation in which something might happen. It can be different for people in long-distance relationships; you might not realize how badly you miss the feel of someone touching your skin until someone reaches out and touches you. Unfortunately, there are people who will prey on you and know you might feel deprived of attention and touch. Do not allow people to take advantage of you and, consequently, to ruin the trust your partner has in you.

Being in a long-distance relationship is an adult decision that takes effort. You made the decision to be with your partner despite the miles, so you also must make the decision not to allow yourself in a situation where your behavior is a contradiction to your decision to be with your partner.

One piece of advice about cheating while in a long-distance relationship: There is a saying that originated from a Bible verse that says what happens in the dark will come to light. Do not think that just because you are miles away from your partner, he or she will not find out if you stray. In today's world of constant monitoring, social networks, and instantaneous dissemination of information, a momentary lapse of judgment can wind up broadcast globally in minutes. That means a single passionate kiss you share with a friend can be common knowledge before you even make it home from your friend's house.

Chapter 6

Flourish Solo and Together

You might feel as though you have two distinctly different lives when you are in a long-distance relationship: the life on your own and the life with your partner. When your partner is not physically around, it can be difficult to integrate your two lives. It is important to pay attention to both lives and to work toward flourishing with and without your partner.

Why is this important? If you are miserable in your solo life (you hate your job; you do not have friends you can rely on; you spend time bored out of your mind), your relationship with your partner inevitably will suffer as well. You need to be happy with yourself and your own life before you can hope to be happy with someone else. The reality of a long-distance relationship is that your partner cannot be there all the time; you need to be able to rely on yourself and have a thriving existence, so you do not feel completely out of control when your partner cannot be there for you.

Avoid the Pity Party

Make no mistake about it: Being in a long-distance relationship can stink. Some days you just want to come home to your partner, fall into his or her arms, and forget the stress of the day. Things can be exponentially harder for people who are left to care for a home, pets, and children while the other partner is away, and thoughts like, "Why am I left to take care of everything?" can invade your mind if you allow them.

So, long-distance relationships can be incredibly hard, and sometimes it might seem like nobody in the world understands the stress. That being said, you made the decision with your partner to stay together despite the distance, and when it comes down to it, being with your partner is worth it even if there are miles between the two of you. Here is the key: Acknowledge that what you are doing is tough, but keep in mind the reasoning behind what you are doing. Your partner is the person you want to be with. Staying together in a long-distance relationship will be one of the hardest things you deal with in your relationship, but in the future, you might look back on it as completely worth the effort. Your relationship will be stronger because the two of you know it can endure time away and still flourish.

Several problems arise when you indulge in a pity party about your current situation. You might become bitter about the distance, which certainly will have an effect on how you deal with your partner. Your pessimism can be infectious, so the next thing you know, you might find yourself dealing with a partner who has fallen into his or her own pity party. Your relationship is going to have a difficult time thriving if the two of you are too busy feeling sorry for yourselves to interact with each other as a couple. You cannot expend the necessary energy to take care of yourself and the emotional needs of your partner if you fall too deeply into a woe-is-me pattern of thinking.

Acknowledge that a long-distance relationship is the result of a choice you made. Consider what compelled you to make that decision in the first place. When it comes down to it, you are not a victim of circumstance, but instead, you are a person who wants to stay with your partner and are willing to endure inconveniences to make it happen. It is terribly romantic when you stop to think about it, and if you can find a way to keep a positive spin on what you are going through, it will help you stay positive and keep everything in perspective.

Again, keep open communication with your partner. If you are frustrated by your circumstances, talk to your partner about your feelings. Just make sure that you do not attack your partner emotionally or bombard him or her with a monologue of whining. Present your feelings, do not throw any blame in your partner's direction, and then listen to what your partner has to say. You might find that your partner feels similarly, and once you realize that being in a long-distance relationship is not easy on either one of you, it might become apparent that your partner is willing to sacrifice for you just as you are willing to sacrifice for him or her. Two people willing to sacrifice for each other is a recipe for success when it comes to just about any relationship, but it is especially true for long-distance relationships.

Tips for Enjoying Solo Time

Just because your partner is miles away does not mean you have to avoid having fun on your own. Having a satisfyingly busy life can translate into feeling more fulfilled even though your partner is away. Find things you enjoy doing, and spend time with positive people who understand what you are going through with your partner away.

Here are tips for making sure you enjoy your own life while you are away from your partner:

- Grant yourself permission to have fun even though your partner cannot join in the fun. A happier you will lead to a better relationship with your partner. If your partner has issues with you going out and having innocent fun, then you need to have a frank discussion with your partner about trust and compromise.

- Find activities that can be done with friends, but also find some activities which are meant to be done alone. Gardening, trips to the library, art classes, and riding bikes along scenic trails are a few examples of the activities you can do that are fun and will not be full of happy couples that remind you of your longing for your partner.

- Consider using the time away from your partner to try some new hobbies or activities that you have wanted to try but have not had the opportunity to do. If you have wanted to write a book, spend your evenings alone as writing time. If you want to take up jogging, set a jogging schedule that will allow you to be in the habit of jogging before your partner returns. Think less of your time away as something you must endure and more as an opportunity to focus on yourself for a while.

- Commit some of your solo time to your relationship. What can you do in your spare time to make your relationship flourish? Whether it is writing letters to your partner, scheduling a flower delivery for your partner's birthday, or painting your bedroom your partner's favorite color, you can do things that will give you a sense of accomplishment and help your relationship thrive. When you do these things, it says to your partner, "I care enough about you to take time out of my free time to make you feel honored and loved."

Tamsen's Tip

Sometimes, it is during my husband's absence that I am most productive with my writing. I can focus more intently on my work while he is away. So, while it is certainly true that I miss him, there can be benefits to the distance, too.

Even though you miss your partner, you still can enjoy life while you are away from each other. As long as you are doing things that will not harm your relationship, being active and content will be better for you and your partner. Wallowing in sadness because you are in a long-distance relationship is not going to do you or your partner any favors. Life is brief, and life does not pause because you and your partner are not physically together. Instead of spending your time waiting for your next visit with your partner, get on with your life and enjoy yourself. When you can enjoy your day-to-day life, you will be poised to deal with the stresses of a long-distance relationship and will rely less on your partner as your sole source of happiness.

Take Care of You and Your Relationship

Keeping a long-distance relationship alive can take effort, and there is a chance your stress levels sometimes can be elevated. It can be easier to deal with the extra stress if you are making an effort to take care of yourself. You also will find that your long-distance relationship will flourish if you put effort into taking care of your relationship as much as you put effort into taking care of yourself. It might sound like significant work and effort, but taking care of yourself and your relationship will be worth it in the end.

Taking care of you

When you get plenty of rest, eat right, and get enough exercise, you feel better altogether, even if you are not in a long-distance relationship. Taking care of yourself allows you to be the best you can be, and if your goal is to flourish in your relationship, then putting effort into your best interests will give you the energy you need to put your best efforts toward your relationship.

Your emotions

Some people lose themselves when they get into a relationship, and when the relationship is a long-distance one, it can be a confusing time. It is common to experience a bit of sadness occasionally during this time; you might feel envy, which displays itself as sadness when you see other happy couples enjoying each other's company. You might find yourself feeling lonely, particularly at night when you know other people are spending time with their loved ones, and you are not able to be physically near your partner. You need to monitor your emotions constantly while you are in a long-distance relationship. If you feel depressed, try to pinpoint from where that particular feeling is coming. If you find yourself feeling gloomy, do not just dismiss the feelings as "feeling blue," and then ignore the sadness. Instead, figure out where the gloominess is coming from and what you can do about it.

This might sound easier said than done, but with practice, you can teach yourself to be in touch with your feelings, so you do not fall into the trap of wallowing in negative emotions. The trick is to analyze your negative emotions the moment they arise. You do not have to be a trained psychoanalyst to do this, but you do have to be willing to be honest with yourself about how you feel.

Here is how it works: When you realize you are experiencing a negative emotion, such as sadness, anger, or frustration, take a mental step back, and figure out why you are experiencing those feelings. Instead of "I'm just having a bad day today," it should be more along the lines of, "I am frustrated because I missed a call from my partner last night, and this frustration is putting me in a tense mood." The power behind recognizing the root of your emotions is that it helps you stop the negative behavior and then try to turn your emotions around. If you can recognize that your tense mood is a direct result of frustration stemming from having missed your partner's phone call the previous night, remind yourself there will be more phone calls from your partner in the future. Your partner probably would not approve of your spending the day in a frustrated rut because you missed a call.

What is the result of this emotional self-analysis? Think about the previous example. Suppose your partner calls, and the first thing you say to him or her is, "I missed your call last night, and today has just been the worst day ever." You are putting the blame on your partner when he or she wanted to chat and just happened to call at a time when you were unavailable. Do this enough and there is a chance your partner will start to associate calling you with the potential for a bad experience, and worse yet, your partner might not even realize that he or she has made this association subconsciously. All your partner will know is that he or she does not feel like calling you anymore.

Now take the same situation, but instead, you say to your partner, "I am sorry I missed your call last night. I was sad that I missed you call, but I am happy to talk to you now." These words change everything dramatically. By telling your partner you were sad to miss the call, but not making it sound like there were major negative repercussions for the missed call, you encourage your partner to keep calling because he or she knows what the phone calls mean to you. When you tell your partner how happy you are to talk to him or her, you set the tone for the rest of the conversation.

It is unlikely that you can take a step back from every emotion and analyze what you are feeling, especially when there are intense emotions involved. On the other hand, if you acquire the ability to acknowledge negative feelings and try to figure out a rational way to view those emotions, you equip yourself to be a better communicator with your partner. You might even become a nicer person to deal with.

What if you just cannot seem to grasp the idea of taking control of your emotions, and you frequently find yourself in a deep depression or fits of rage? When your negative emotions start to have a negative impact on your life, it might be time to seek professional help. Give yourself permission to get the help you need so you can take control of your emotional life. A licensed therapist can give you the coping tools you need to not allow this stressful time in your life to define who you are forever.

Your physical health

Studies point to physical health having a positive impact on emotional well-being. One medical study from the University of Arizona states that there is a direct correlation between exercise and positive mental health. The Mayo Clinic also reveals that people who make time to take care of themselves and include physical activity in their regular routines may experience better moods because of the increased production of chemicals in the brain directly related to mood regulation. This is certainly not to say that people who are fit are always happy, no that people who are not fit spend their days wallowing in grief. Instead, the idea is that physical activity enhances your life in a variety of ways, and one of the benefits can be emotional well-being.

The goal is to take care of your relationship and take care of yourself. This is not an egotistical goal; instead, it is an acknowledgement that you can give more to your partner when you have invested in yourself. Taking time out every day, or a few times a week, so you can take a walk or visit the gym can help you in a wide range of ways. You can make your health better and find that you deal with stress better. Your emotional responses will be more reasonable than they might have otherwise been.

If you are already fit, make sure you stay on course and do not allow your relationship's long-distance arrangement derail your progress. If you are frequently able to travel to see your partner, try not to fall into the trap of gaining weight when you travel.

It can be easy not to pay attention to your caloric intake when you are away from home, and sometimes, these trips to see your partner might feel like mini-vacations where you do not have to worry about what you eat. The problem is when these mini-vacations are relatively frequent because the damage done during these trips can add up.

Tamsen's Tip

When I found out my husband was going away for a year, I wasted no time in tracking down an excellent personal trainer at a local gym. I knew that if I was going to deal with the stress of having my husband away, raising two kids, and maintaining my writing career, it was essential to make time for exercise. Having a personal trainer helped keep me accountable, and as a bonus, when my husband returned, I was in better shape than when he left.

If you are not fit, consider using this time away from your partner as an excellent opportunity to take control of your health. Start small with daily walks after dinner, or invest in exercise DVDs that you can do at home. If joining a gym is financially feasible, find a gym close to home or work and try to attend group fitness classes or even spend time with a personal trainer. It does not take long to see results when you dedicate time to getting in shape, especially if you are intentional and dedicated to the process.

There is more than one reason to get serious about your physical health, but when it comes right down to it, taking care of yourself is one of the important things you can do in a long-distance relationship to ensure you are at your best. It is easier to deal with the stresses of having a partner who is not physically around if you get regular exercise and eat right, and you poise yourself to give more to your partner when you have first given to yourself.

CASE STUDY: EXPERT ADVICE

Dr. Amber Tyler

Chronic stress is actually very hard on the body. Aside from the emotional effects people typically think of such as anxiety, depression, and sleep problems, a whole host of physical symptoms can occur. Chronic stress can raise your blood pressure. It increases your risk for heart disease and diabetes. It can affect digestion, causing acid reflux (heartburn), constipation, or diarrhea. When you are under a lot of stress, your muscles tend to be tenser, which triggers headaches and muscular pains such as back pain, shoulder pain, etc. Stress increases the likelihood that you will clench or grind your teeth in your sleep, which causes problems with your jaw and can cause broken teeth. People who are under chronic stress generally experience an overall higher level of pain.

Stress triggers a "fight or flight" response, which is very beneficial for sudden stressful situations such as an attack on your safety or a tornado, but not very beneficial as a perpetual condition. When you experience chronic stress, your body lives in the "fight or flight" response all the time, though to a lesser degree than in sudden intense situations. This means that your body is making and circulating increased levels of stress hormones, especially cortisol. This has a lot of impact on the body. It impacts the immune system, making you more vulnerable to illness. It can contribute to cravings for sugary and fatty foods (comfort foods) and increases the conversion of things we eat into stored fat, so you gain weight.

The good news is that even if you cannot remove or change the source of your chronic stress, you can do something to counteract the effects. Exercise is the best medicine available for many health conditions, but especially for people under stress. Exercise increases your body's production of endorphins, a "feel good" chemical. Endorphins reduce symptoms associated with anxiety and depression, decrease pain levels, and boost your immune system. Exercise lowers your blood pressure, improves your body's processing of sugars (decreasing the risk of diabetes), and lowers cholesterol. People who exercise regularly fall asleep faster and sleep better than those who do not exercise. Exercise also helps people attain and maintain a healthy weight, which makes everyone feel better physically and emotionally.

There are so many ways to exercise that everyone should be able to find something. It can range from the traditional running or aerobics classes to something like a dance game on the Nintendo® Wii™ or Xbox® Kinect™ (Those games can burn a lot of calories.). If you can afford it, joining a gym and consulting with a trainer can be useful because you are accountable to someone, and you want to get your money's worth. Take a martial arts class, yoga, pole dancing — whatever you can find that you will enjoy. If you can find a friend to do it with you, you will be more likely to continue because they can get you going on days you may have otherwise talked yourself out of working out. Then, you need to set goals, and they need to be reasonable goals. Do not start running with plans of training for a marathon; that is overwhelming, and it is easy to get discouraged and quit. A better goal in the beginning is something like exercising for 15 to 20 minutes three times a week. That is much more manageable. Once you have turned that goal into a habit, set a new goal, something like 30 minutes of exercise, five times a week. Gradually increase until you get where you want to be.

If you have a chronic health problem such as high blood pressure, heart disease, or a joint disorder, you should see your doctor before beginning an exercise program to determine what is the safest and most effective way for you to exercise. Very few people cannot exercise in some way. If you are otherwise healthy, then the most important first step is to find something you think is fun. If you do not like what you are doing, it is unlikely that you will stick with it.

Your relationship's health

You already know how important it is to take care of your emotional and physical health so that you can give your best to your partner. You also need to realize that your relationship needs to be cultivated and cared for, too. Just as you care for yourself because you know it is important, concentrate effort into taking care of your relationship.

This is different from taking care of your partner. Try to visualize your relationship as a separate entity; although it is true that your relationship is not necessarily a living, breathing thing, it is something that needs attention and can easily fade away if it is not given sufficient attention. Couples who have traditional relationships can fall into an easy pattern of cultivating their relationships without even realizing they are doing so, but when you are in a long-distance relationship, it can take concerted effort.

Start by asking yourself this question: "How can I improve the health of my relationship with my partner?" You might already know you can do one thing to make your partner feel better about the relationship and another thing to make you feel better about the relationship, but what can you do that will benefit both of you, thereby contributing to the health of the relationship?

Here is an example: Suppose you have the opportunity to go to a conference for work, which is in the same city as your boyfriend's parents. You have never met his parents, and as far as you are concerned, it would be an awkward meeting, especially considering he would not be present. Your partner tells you it is up to you whether you meet with his parents, so there is no pressure from him regarding what decision to make. When you examine the situation from an outside perspective, however, you realize that meeting your partner's parents would strengthen your relationship for more than one reason. Your partner might take it as a compliment that you took the time to meet them. The parents might take it as a sign of respect that you put time aside from your work schedule to meet them. As a bonus, you would get a sneak peek at people who might someday be your in-laws. The decision to meet with your boyfriend's parents while away for a conference would benefit the relationship. This was not a decision you made because your partner urged you to or because you had a burning desire to meet your partner's parents, but instead, you made the decision because you knew it would be best for your relationship as a whole.

You will encounter a wide variety of situations in which you have to decide what is best for your relationship when there is no clear benefit or drawback for you or your partner. When faced with these types of scenarios, ask yourself if there is a benefit to your relationship as a whole. Along those same lines, when faced with a decision that might have negative consequences to your relationship, think twice before forging ahead.

Communication, partnered with decision-making that always looks toward the best interests of the relationship, will help your long-distance relationship flourish.

Support from Others

Consider yourself fortunate if you have a large network of friends and family who are available to support you. People in long-distance relationships often can feel isolated socially because they are not able to enjoy the same day-to-day interactions with partners that people in traditional relationships enjoy. If you have friends who make sure you still enjoy going out and having fun in a social setting, this can help you stave off feelings of being alone while your partner is miles away.

On the other hand, it is a delicate balance. You do not want to rely on other people so much that you start to become needy, and you certainly do not want to fall into a pattern of turning to other people to fulfill you emotionally (particularly people of the opposite sex). Even if your partner is several time zones away, he or she should still be the one person who most fulfills you emotionally.

Family and close friends should offer you support and socialization. They should encourage you to still get out and have fun, but they should not encourage you to do things that would sabotage your relationship. It should be understood among all your friends and family that you are in a committed relationship, and just because you and your partner are not physically together does not mean you are available. Make sure you surround yourself with people who are on board with your relationship and who will not speak badly about your partner or your situation. It can be difficult to be in a long-distance relationship if the people around you are not supportive of the arrangement because you do not get the daily affirmation of hugging your partner at the end of the day. If you listen to enough negative talk from people close to you, you might start to accept it as truth.

Ask for help from the people you trust. If you have children and need someone else to give you a break occasionally, do not be apprehensive about asking someone else to take the children and give you a breather. If there is nobody in your family or social circle that is able or willing to take your children, pets, or help you in other ways, seek out the help of someone you can pay for this help.

Tamsen's Tip

I use SitterCity (**www.sittercity.com**), which is a website that has listings of local babysitters, pet sitters, house sitters, and people who will run errands. You can read profiles and review background checks before hiring someone. Other websites offer similar services; so have a look around and take advantage of the Internet when trying to find help.

Asking for help is not a sign of weakness. If you cannot seem to manage keeping up with your housework, consider bringing in a cleaning crew on a regular basis. If you cannot keep up with your lawn, think about hiring someone to mow your grass once a week. The idea is to not get overwhelmed with the tasks you have to handle on your own. For some people, maintaining everything is no big deal because they have never lived with their partners, so they are accustomed to dealing with everything by themselves. If, on the other hand, your long-distance arrangement is temporary and you are used to having your partner around to split responsibilities with, seek out and accept help when possible.

Whether your help comes from your family, friends, or someone you pay to help you, the point is to take the burden off you. This might come in the form of a friend who meets you for coffee once a week, a relative who comes over and helps you fold laundry, or someone you pay to walk your dog while you are at work. Recognize what areas of your life could use help, and figure out a way to ask for the help you need.

Do not discount your partner's ability to help you from miles away. You might find that your partner happily will make phone calls, research things online, or take other tasks off your hands that are filling up your calendar but that you do not have to accomplish on your own. Your partner's ability to help you with tasks will differ depending on his or her situation and the tasks you need done, but do not immediately disregard your partner as a source for help.

In fact, he or she should be your primary source of emotional support. This can be easier said than done when you are in a long-distance relationship, but as long as you keep the lines of communication open and accurately portray your need for emotional support to your partner, then it can be done. Keep in mind the old saying that "distance makes the heart grow fonder;" distance does not compel people to stop caring about their partner's emotional needs. If your partner stops caring about your emotional needs just because there are miles separating the two of you, then there are bigger problems that need to be addressed.

CASE STUDY:
ASKING FOR HELP

Detra, military spouse and mom

We had been in a foreign country for a short time before my husband had to leave for a deployment, so I did not have a support system. This was stressful at first. I even thought about going home, but I do not have any real family to speak of, and it would have cost too much money in flights, a second rent, furniture, and loss of the housing allowance the military gives us, so I stayed. People came out of the woodwork to help me. Coworkers of my husband took me on girls' nights out, took my family bowling, and things like that. My neighbor and her husband took care of all the "man jobs" that I could not figure out. I even got a fantastic job, so I would not go crazy while my hubby was gone. I still have the job, have found a love for what I do, and might like to continue when I get back to the States.

My biggest supporter was my teenage son. He stepped up and helped me. He was a surrogate dad to the little ones and made sure I got away occasionally. He was my adult conversation and a smile when I needed one. I am honestly not sure how I could have made it without him.

The most difficult thing about being separated was the waiting. There was this constant feeling of waiting, and time moved so slowly. Second was having help with the children — not the chores but just someone to help with the emotions of being a parent of four children. I missed having someone to help comfort them and someone to listen to how my day was at the end of the day. I also missed having someone to share the joys of life with and someone to tell the funny things the children did.

There were benefits to my husband being away. I had complete control over my time. I also had about three hours a day to myself after the chil- dren went to bed. It was divine. Normally, my entire life is spent meeting everyone else's needs, so this was huge. Also, I got to know myself; I found out what I would be like on my own, and I found I was a better person than I had imagined: smarter, more competent, more ef- ficient, and a better housekeeper. I did not procrastinate on housework because I knew I was the only one who was going to do it, and I could only blame myself.

I began being more organized as a mom out of necessity. The children learned to pick up after themselves for the first time and learned to help with things, such as setting the table, doing dishes, and taking out the trash. This has kept up even though my husband has been back for more than a year now, and our family runs a bit smoother because of it.

Chapter 7

The Long-Distance Date

Just because you and your partner are not physically together does not mean that you cannot commit time to each other occasionally. The concept of a date — long-distance or otherwise — is to get time together and concentrate effort on staying connected. Although this preferably is done while physically together, a date certainly can occur long distance.

Now is a convenient time to be in a long-distance relationship. As long as you have the technological capabilities and know how to pull it off, you can have dates with your partner who is miles away but still feel like the two of you are in the same room. That is the beauty of webcam chats and similar technology; you can see your partner and see his or her surroundings while he or she can see your surroundings. There does not have to be any mystery about where your partner is calling you from or what coffee shop you are sitting in because with webcam technology, your partner can see everything that is around you and in the span of the webcam. This certainly can help the two of you feel more connected.

Even if you do not have the ability to use a webcam or similar technology, other options are available. The point is to make a concerted effort to spend time together when your attention is not on something else. This is a time when the two of you concentrate on each other and try to connect as best as you can, even while apart.

Not an Impossible Feat

Having a date with your partner who is away from you is possible, even though it might seem cheesy or awkward at times. To say, "I have a date with my partner" and then sit down in front of a laptop's webcam at your kitchen table can feel odd, but once you get used to this method of "dating," you will soon find that these sessions can help the two of you feel closer. It is nice to know your partner will drop everything else and clear his or her schedule to spend time with you — even if that time is not physically together, it can help strengthen the bond between the two of you.

Figure out what works best for your relationship. Is there a specific day and time that will work every week, or do your sporadic schedules make it impossible to know from one week to the next when you can spend virtual time together? Set a start time and end time for your date. You can adjust the end time of your date if the two of you are having a discussion or are enjoying each other's company too much to stop, but when two people live apart it is common for them both to have separate schedules and obligations. An end time for the date makes the entire process less daunting; a busy partner does not have to worry that the virtual date will drag on, particularly if there is still work to be done or if the time difference forces the date to happen late at night for one person.

Commit to a certain number of dates per week or month, if possible. This might be difficult for couples who have busy schedules or who cannot plan ahead because of other obligations, but if it works out to have a preset time and day for your date, then it is something you can look forward to and anticipate. Do not feel pressure to entertain your partner on your dates; this is simply a time to dedicate to each other and to hang out — as much as two people can "hang out" when miles away from each other.

If you are intentional about setting time aside for your date, no matter how often or what form your date takes, this will help keep the two of you connected while also keeping the lines of communication open. For a long-distance relationship, these benefits are gold.

Date versus chat

There is a difference between an everyday chat on the phone or computer with your partner and a date to chat on the phone or computer. The difference is that a date is intentional; the time has been set aside, and it is understood that this specific time is intended for the two of you to spend time together. When you just happen to reach your partner to say hello, you might call or instant message at a time when your partner is not able to give you exclusive attention, or you might call or instant message at a time when your partner is trying to get something else done. When a date has been set, you both know the focus should be solely on your partner and the things you want to talk about. When the conversation is a date, it takes precedence over everything else at that time.

These dates can be precious. When you are in a long-distance relationship, you can lose sight of why you allow yourself to be in this situation. You might wonder if the relationship is truly worth the extra effort. When your partner is willing — and perhaps even eager — to set time aside to spend time with you (even though it is not time physically spent together), it helps to remind you of how special your relationship is.

This is not to say that impromptu conversations are not of value, but there is also value in scheduling time together. Think of it this way: If the two of you lived under the same roof and saw each other every day, you would still make plans to go out on dates together. There is just something about setting time aside to be together. You do not have to plan to do spectacular things on your date; just be together.

Types of Dates

The types of dates you manage to have with your partner long-distance are more plentiful than you might realize. As long as you both have telephone and Internet capabilities, you might find that you can even vary the dating methods you try. This can be beneficial particularly if one or both or you do not feel comfortable with talking on the phone or chatting online because it allows you to explore different methods and decide which one works best for you.

Start out by designating a certain time and day for your date. Make sure it is a time and day when there are few or no distractions. Depending on where you are both located, you might want to vary the location that each of you goes to for the date. For example, both of you going to a coffee shop in your respective cities and talking to each other via phone or computer can make you feel less apart.

The telephone date

Make sure your logistics are out of the way before your telephone date. You want to ensure that a day and time has been set and that your phone is fully charged. Decide beforehand who will call whom, so there is no confusion. You might want to consider turning off call waiting on your phone for the duration of your date because it can be annoying to try to have a conversation over the phone that is being interrupted constantly. Even if you do not click over to the other line to answer the call, there is still the annoying beep on your end and what sounds like a pause on the other end, or vice versa. One of the biggest points of a phone date is to help your long-distance partner feel as though he or she has your undivided attention for a time. Call waiting interrupt-

ing your conversation is a reminder to both of you of the limitations you have as a couple to be allowed time together without distance getting in the way.

What should you talk about on your phone date? Try to avoid the mundane things that get inserted into everyday conversation. This is not the time to talk about how the toilet overflowed or how your boss is driving you crazy. Talk about things that will help the two of you feel better connected, such as reasons why you love each other, what your plans are for the future together, or anything else that is a mutual topic that both of you easily can participate in chatting about.

Some long-distance couples get a kick out of sharing experiences throughout the week and then talking about them on phone dates. For example, reading the same book at the same pace, such as a chapter a night, and then discussing the book over the phone can help keep the two of you connected. This does not have to be a relationship book that the two of you read but, instead, can be anything that appeals to both of you. Find something that will hold your attention and the attention of your partner. You do not want to force a book on your partner that he or she will resent having to read, especially something along the lines of a self-help book if your partner does not feel the need to self-improve and sees the command to read the book as a dig.

Watching favorite TV shows or a movie together on a phone date can be fun, too. This is easy if you live in similar time zones or if you have the capability to access shows in other ways, such as online, on DVR, or DVD. For couples that share an interest in a certain show, this is a way to feel closer. Miles might separate the two of you, but you can still have shared experiences.

Tamsen's Tip

Find out what your calling plan is on your phone. Long-distance relationships can result in significant time spent chatting on the phone, so it helps if you know what hours you get free calling or how many minutes you have in a given month. Otherwise, exuberant phone conversations can lead to a ridiculously huge phone bill at the end of the month.

Telecommuting kisses

There is a chance you have one of two stances on the concept of phone sex. You might think it is an excellent way to feel closer to your partner when the two of you cannot physically be together, or conversely, you might consider it embarrassing. It might be something you want to try but are not sure how to broach the subject with your partner. Although it might be easy to speak frankly about emotions to get your point across, such as saying, "I feel sad that you are gone," it is a different thing to propose a session of phone sex with your partner when the two of you have not gone that route before. This is one category where it might be best to allow these types of conversations to occur naturally. If you are talking about the weather one minute and then in the next breath you tell your partner you want to engage in phone sex, it can be likened to having a face-to-face conversation with your partner about mopping the kitchen floor and then suddenly saying, "By the way, let's go get busy in the bedroom." Some people need more buildup to feel amorous.

If phone sex makes you feel uncomfortable — or downright icky — then tell your partner how you feel and assure your partner it has nothing to do with how you feel about him or her. Reveal that you just feel weird engaging in phone sex and that it is not something you enjoy. This is not to say that you will never want to try phone sex, and perhaps someday it just will happen, but if your partner knows it is not something you enjoy, then you can save some awkward conversations.

If you want to give phone sex a try, but you are not sure how to broach the subject with your partner, you have different options. There is the frank suggestion, such as, "Do you want to give phone sex a try?" Or there is the option of trying to steer the conversation into a sensual direction and seeing where it goes from there. If you find that your attempts at hinting to your partner are not working well, you might want to try something more blatant, such as, "I am lying in bed right now, and I am pretending you are here. What are you doing to me?" This type of talk should be eased into and happen in the context of the conversation. You might just confuse your partner if you leap from one topic into suddenly going heavy on the sexual talk.

If phone sex is something that you and your partner enjoy, you might find that it is something you regularly plan on and might even be the focus of your phone dates. If this is the case, plan ahead and make it a real event; make your phone call from your bedroom, your bathtub, or whatever gets you in the mood. Two consenting adults who engage in phone sex can find that it is the best substitute possible until they can be physically together again.

The Internet date

The Internet offers options for virtual dates with your partner. Whether you want to chat with your partner via webcam or instant message with your partner for your date, the conversations happen in real time and can happen anywhere you have an Internet connection.

Skype is one of the best bets for a long-distance date, but it is not foolproof. If one or both of you have slow Internet connections, the chat might be more frustrating than anything else because the screen can slow down or freeze, and the sound quality can become distorted. The norm, however, is that the webcam technology works fine, and the quality of the picture and sound makes the conversation pleasant.

After the two of you have decided on a day and time, figure out the logistics beforehand, just as you would for a telephone date. Are the two of you going to set up your laptops in specified places, such as at home or coffee shops? Make sure that wherever you set up, you have a connection to the Internet. Depending on the capabilities you and your partner have on your cell phones, you might be able to use the Internet to chat with video using your phones, but if that is your plan, then check beforehand to test the picture and make sure it works. You might find that your laptop is the best bet for video chat, but again, this depends on the technology at your disposal.

If you use a portable modem for your Internet connection, check beforehand to find out if you have a limited number of minutes online before additional charges are incurred. If you plan to use Skype or a similar program, install this program ahead of time, and test it before the day your online date arrives. If your partner logs on to chat with you, and you do not show up online until 20 minutes later because you were downloading the program, he or she might wonder how committed to the process you are if you did not think to download the program beforehand.

If you are going to be in full sight of your partner because you are using a webcam for your Internet date, take time to spruce yourself up beforehand just as you would with a face-to-face date. Also, pay attention to your surroundings; no matter how much you dress yourself up before sitting down in front of the computer, if you are sitting in a messy room because you have not bothered to clean your house, this is going to detract from the quality of the conversation. Remove anything in the webcam's view that might distract your partner, and have some compassion for your partner if he or she is far away and missing the comforts of home. For example, if the two of you love a particular restaurant, but this restaurant is not available where your partner is, do not sit in front of the webcam slurping on a to-go cup from that restaurant. Your goal for your Internet date is to feel connected to your partner, not to remind your partner about the distance between the two of you.

This should go without saying, but it is important and needs to be mentioned: Your Internet date via webcam is not an appropriate time to have friends pop up and wave at your partner, especially if these friends are of the opposite sex, because your partner might view this as a threat. Imagine chatting with your partner online, and suddenly someone else shows up on the webcam, smiling and waving at you but with one arm around your partner. No matter how innocently this is intended, there is a chance that damage can be done. Your partner should walk away from the webcam conversation feeling closer to you instead of walking away from the conversation feeling as though someone else is threatening your relationship.

Your Internet date should focus on you and your partner. Do not allow yourself to get distracted by other things; if your partner is trying to talk to you via webcam, and your eyes keep darting back and forth to something out of your partner's range of sight, your partner might wonder what you are looking at that is so important and might even become annoyed at your apparent lack of interest in the conversation. You might not intend it that way, and perhaps you are only looking at your cat jumping up on a bookcase or something equally distracting, but unless you explain this to your partner, then there is no way for him or her to know what is going on.

Amorous video

Think twice before engaging in sexual behavior via webcam. In the heat of the moment, you might think of it as a way to feel closer to your partner, but when it comes right down to it, you are performing in front of a camera. Even if you think your Internet connection is 100-percent secure, and even if you know that you can trust your partner, many other variables can turn the entire event into a public matter.

It is too easy for a screenshot of your webcam conversation to wind up in the wrong hands. You cannot know for sure that someone else is not tapped into your Internet connection (or your partner's Internet connection), so privacy is not guaranteed when having a webcam conversation. For this reason, it is best to avoid shedding any clothing while in front of a webcam, no matter how much you miss your partner.

Internet chatting

Webcam is not your only option for an Internet date. Whether you or your partner feels uncomfortable in front of a webcam, or if webcam capabilities are limited for you or your partner, instant messaging can make for interesting long-distance date. The same rules apply for an instant messaging date as they would for any other long-distance date: Set a time and day beforehand,

and make sure that the time set aside is solely for the two of you to connect and feel closer. If instant messaging is new to you, install the program long beforehand, and try it out before the date. Great options for instant messaging (IM) include Yahoo!® Messenger and Facebook, although plenty of other options are available. Talk to your partner about his or her preferences and decide on which IM program you will use together; if either of you will instant message from work or from overseas, options might be limited because sometimes these programs are blocked by firewalls because of security reasons.

If you and your partner want to add a level of playfulness to your dates, consider trying out one of the many "virtual worlds" available online. These websites allow you to create your own character and wander around the "world" chatting with other people. Your avatar and your partner's avatar can meet up in exotic online locations and play games together or have conversations. Check out IMVU® (**www.imvu.com**) or a similar online world to see if this is a good option for you and your partner.

Making dates work

Even in today's modern age of technological advancements, not everyone has ready access to computers or telephones. This can be true especially for people who serve in the military in remote locations or for people with other limitations that make it impossible to set time aside for a virtual date. In these instances, it is important to work with what you have and try to find a way to stay connected despite the limitations.

Get creative in these situations. If your only option for communication with your partner is through the postal mail, sit down regularly to compose letters that are meaningful and help bring the two of you closer together. Consider these letters your "dates" until you have the ability to connect in other ways. The point of the long-distance date is to give you a chance to focus on your partner and vice versa, so if all you can do is write letters to accomplish this, make the letters your focus for the time being. The fact that you still make an effort to connect with your partner long distance despite the limitations in your way makes it even more apparent to your partner that you are committed to making the relationship work.

Chapter 8

Visiting Time

Not all long-distance couples get the opportunity to have time face-to-face, but for these relationships to flourish, there has to be time together at some point. Even if the visits are rare, coming together and spending time physically together is an important occurrence that will refresh you and your partner. Something about having your partner standing in front of you instead of in front of a webcam helps you remember why you put up with a long-distance arrangement in the first place. Time together helps you reconnect with all the emotions you have when your partner embraces you, smiles at you, and is just there with you.

Negotiating Time Together

If you hope to flourish in your long-distance relationship, it is vitally important that you both make time for each other. While apart, make time to chat over the phone, send email messages, or use whatever form of communication is easiest and preferred between the two of you. In addition to this long-distance time together, you must make time to see each other face to face. Although it is true that you might be able to maintain a relationship without seeing each other face to face, when the goal is to go beyond "maintaining" and into "flourishing," visits have to be a part of the overall equation.

Finding ways to spend time together physically can be incredibly challenging. You have to consider each other's schedules, traveling preferences, and financial situations. You might have a burning desire to go visit your partner for the holidays, but then when you check airline ticket prices you find that you cannot afford the price of the tickets. You may have the financial resources necessary to go visit your partner, but your work schedule or other obligations makes it impossible to get away. Maybe you have enough money and an abundance of time, but you are terrified of traveling.

Whatever the reason, there is a good chance you will encounter obstacles that have to be overcome in order to spend some time with your partner face-to-face (or to have your partner come visit you). Keep in mind that the effort you put forth to overcome the obstacles will be worth it if your main goal is to flourish in your relationship.

Dealing with the logistics that come along with planning a visit with your partner becomes absolutely worth the effort. Negotiate with your partner to figure out the answers to these questions:

- How often should we physically see each other? Ideally, visits should be a recurring event. Although this might not be possible for some situations, if it is possible to have recurring visits, this should be a priority.

- What financial changes should we make in order to make frequent visits possible? Travel can be expensive, whether it entails driving a few hours in a car or taking numerous flights to a final destination. Even if the two of you keep your finances separate, this is one area where you should work together to figure out how to set money aside so visits can be frequent.

- How can we overcome any other obstacles to make frequent visits possible? The obstacles you encounter might be different than what other couples encounter, just as your definition of "frequent" may vary from what other people consider frequent. The goal is to overcome whatever obstacles you encounter as a couple and to overcome these obstacles together.

You might find that your partner's preference for frequency of visits is different from your own preference. This is one instance when it is important to not only recognize that you are both individuals with your own preferences, but also to recognize that compromise is a vital aspect of any relationship. Warning flags should appear in your mind if your partner refuses to make any plans for any visits, even in the future. It is one thing to not be able to visit because of travel costs or packed schedules, but it is another thing entirely to not want to visit a partner.

If you find that your attempt at negotiating time together results in your partner saying something along the lines of "Why should we bother? Everything is great the way it is," then this should be a warning sign that your relationship is far from flourishing. It is true that some people are drawn to long-distance relationships because of the independence it allows them. This does not automatically equal a doomed relationship, but it can result in one or both partners become complacent and not trying to put forth the appropriate effort to help the relationship thrive. *You will learn more about figuring out whether or not your relationship is worth the effort in Chapter 10.*

Cherishing Time Together

However, if your relationship is growing and thriving appropriately, there will come a time when you and your partner will meet face-to-face. For some couples, the long-distance relationship is a temporary arrangement. Other couples find themselves perpetually apart, with visits scheduled whenever their finances and calendars allow. Even for couples that meet online, court from afar, and maintain their long-distance relationship with no real end to the distance in sight, there should be some time that can be spent together in the same room. Do not underestimate the power of time spent together that will not only refresh your fortitude to stay together and stay committed but also may reveal some interesting things about your partner that you might not have realized otherwise.

While your involuntary inclination might be to try to pack a bunch of activities into your time together in an attempt to make up for all the time apart, resist this urge. Your time with your partner should be as calm as possible for both your sakes. What qualifies as "calm" is different for each couple; talk to your partner to find out what you can do together that not only will be fun, but also will allow the two of you to enjoy time together. Remember that time with your partner becomes even more precious when you are in a long-distance relationship. Just something about knowing that your partner (or you) will have to leave after a certain amount of time makes the time you do have together seem all that more important.

Avoid unrealistic expectations

Whether this is the first time you will be in the same room with your long-distance partner or if this is one of many scheduled visits the two of you share, it is common for people to plan frantically for what they expect to be the "perfect" visit. In their minds, the perfect visit includes a wonderful time had by both partners, in which there are no strained conversations that evolve into arguments, and plenty of time is spent gazing into each other's eyes and sighing in contentment. Unfortunately, life rarely works this way, particularly when two human beings are involved. You can never know if your partner will show up grumpy, if you will have a raging headache, or if the two of you have problems easing into a comfortable groove.

Problems arise when you or your partner have unrealistic expectations for what the visit will entail. This certainly does not mean you should not eagerly anticipate the visit or that you should not plan any fun activities with your partner. Instead, what it means is that you do not tell yourself that if everything does not go smoothly then there must be something wrong with your relationship (or with you, or with your partner). Do not allow these cognitive leaps to ruin your visit and, perhaps, eventually lead to the end of your relationship. Cognitive leaps happen when your mind jumps from one statement to a conclusion, yet the two do not necessarily make sense when looked at logically. In this example, the cognitive leap is from one statement ("This visit is not going as smoothly as I had planned.") to a conclusion that is probably not logical ("Our relationship is doomed."). It might make sense in your head, but when you actually examine your thinking, you will realize the two things probably are not even connected.

Talk to your partner before the visit to find out what he or she expects, and then talk about what you expect. It is far better to discover beforehand that your partner is hoping for a quiet, relaxing trip, especially if you were planning in your mind a busy weekend complete with a packed schedule of parties and activities and hardly any time for the two of you just to be together. Come to a happy compromise beforehand; make it clear what you both hope to do throughout your time together, and your visit will likely go much more smoothly than it would have otherwise.

Not surprisingly, it all comes down to open communication. Talking to your partner about what you both expect for the visit can avoid a great deal of frustration when the time actually comes to see each other. Just like other facets of a successful long-distance relationship, quite a bit hinges on whether the two of you are clear about your expectations, hopes, and fears. If one of you is hoping for an incredibly romantic visit with almost all time spent together while the other partner is hoping for a busy weekend visiting a wide variety of friends, problems are going to arise if expectations are not discussed and a compromise put into place. In this particular instance, both you and your partner might be able to enjoy the visit if time intentionally is set aside for romance and additional time set aside for visiting friends.

Keep in mind that the visit is not all about you. You might fall into a trap of about what you want and need for the visit and forget to talk to your partner about what he or she wants. Many people do this without even realizing they are doing it. Even if your partner tells you to go ahead and take the reins in planning, this should not mean the visit is all about what you want without taking into consideration your partner's preferences. Plan your visits to be mutually beneficial for both you and your partner.

Accept that it is quite unlikely your visit is going to be perfect. You also may want to have some moments of reflection to figure out what a "perfect" visit looks like for you and to recognize aspects within your ideal visit that are not realistic. Do you envision a visit without a single disagreement? When two people get together for a visit, especially when there are emotions involved, there is a good chance you will need to talk through at least one or two things. Whether it is a decision of which movie to see or where your relationship is going, you might have moments during your visit in which you have to talk something through with your partner. You might think these disagreements are signs that your relationship is in trouble, but to the contrary, disagreements can be healthy when they are resolved mutually.

If you and your partner do not see each other often — or if your visit is the first time the two of you have ever been in the same room together because you met online — allow for some awkwardness. Again, this is another instance where you cannot permit cognitive leaps to make initial awkwardness equal a doomed relationship. You are two individuals who have two separate lives, and it is only natural to have some moments of awkwardness when you first get together for a visit. This is not an automatic sign that the two of you do not belong together; it is a sign that the two of you are two individuals, and that is a good thing. Work through the awkwardness together, and your relationship will be stronger in the end.

CASE STUDY:
HOW TO MAKE IT WORK

Emily, currently in a
long-distance relationship

It is difficult to be so far from someone you are trying to get to know and to determine if he or she is the person you want to spend the rest of your life with. It would be nice to get to see each other more regularly. When you do not get to see someone on a regular basis, you cannot see how that person acts and reacts in situations that come up. Spending limited time together gets to be tough. It would be nice to be able to just call each other up and say "Hey, meet me here or there for dinner tonight. I would love to see you." At times, I get jealous of couples that do have the option of doing that. We talk on the phone every day, but there is something to be said for actually "seeing" and physically being with that person.

Long-distance relationships also can be expensive. Being states away from the person I am dating means paying airfares or spending money on tanks of gas to get to see him. If you are both on a limited income, it can be quite challenging. It can be stressful not knowing when you will get to see the other person again. And when you are together, you want to get out and experience all sorts of things together — movies, sporting events, local attractions — they all cost money.

Communication is key. In a past long-distance relationship, things fizzled out due to a lack of communication and a lack of a planning for when we would see each other again. Although it is important to communicate often, it is still important to keep yourself in touch with local friends and family members. This is probably important for all kinds of relationships; do not fall into the habit of spending all your time and energy on just the person you are dating. You need to stay connected with family and friends. They are your support systems whether your relationship is long distance or local.

Initial awkwardness

Couples meeting for the first time, or couples who are readying to see each other face-to-face for the first time in a while, generally accept there will be some initial awkwardness when they are finally able to see each other. For some people, the awkwardness appears as a type of nervousness while for others it comes out as a giddiness that resembles the "butterflies in the stomach" that is commonplace in the beginning stages of a new relationship. Whether positive or negative, couples who can accept the initial awkwardness, be open about their feelings, and do not jump to the conclusion that awkwardness always has to mean something bad, probably will enjoy successful visits that serve to strengthen the relationship overall.

Assuming there will be no awkwardness can be a mistake. Although awkwardness is not necessarily inevitable, it also should come to a shock to even the most seasoned couples. Couples that have been together for a long time but that were geographically separated for work or other reasons for an extended time might struggle with awkwardness because they fear the presence of awkwardness translates into a sign of bigger problems. For example, suppose a couple that has been married for several years, has children together, and has no serious problems within the relationship is forced into a long-distance relationship for whatever reason (military deployment, staying with an ailing family member, etc.). The long-distance relationship goes on for a significant amount of time, such as six months or a year. When the two of them finally are able to be back together, they might not anticipate any awkwardness at all because, after all, they have been married for years and have a thriving life together. In instances such as these, any awkwardness that appears might cause alarm between one or both of the people trying to ease back into their life together.

It is important to keep in mind that physical distance can change a person's perception of touch. Suppose your partner has been away for months on end, and throughout those months, you hardly have been touched by anyone of the opposite gender with the exception of occasional hugs or handshakes. Many people have the tendency to form a "bubble" around themselves in which they are seldom touched and might become accustomed to this. When your partner arrives for a visit or comes home after an extended time away, you might need a little time before you can delve back into physical intimacy. After an extended period without intimacy — even if you have been with your partner for many years — you might find you need to take things slowly.

If this is the case, be clear about your intentions. After all, your partner might not feel the same need for patience when it comes to intimacy, so if you reject physical advances without explaining your reasons, there are bound to be problems. This can be a delicate balance. On one hand, you want things to go at your own pace, and you want to be comfortable, but on the other hand, you want to be sensitive to the desires and needs of your partner. Open communication is the solution. Say "I need a little time to ease back into being physical with you," or "Let's take things slowly because I haven't been touched in months," or whatever else will clearly convey your needs without leaving questions unanswered. Imagine how you would feel if you were trying to be intimate with your partner after a long absence and he or she refused without explanation. What a whirlwind of questions and suspicions that would create within your mind. Avoid this problem by saying what you are feeling and what you need.

Tamsen's Tip

Be your own advocate. If you are not comfortable with physical intimacy with your partner (whether the two of you have been together for years or if this is the first time meeting face-to-face) you need to stand up for yourself. Giving in will result in an intimate experience in which you feel as though you have betrayed your own best interests, and this is not healthy for you or your relationship. On the other hand, perpetually refusing intimacy when there has been intimacy in the past is going to cause problems unless this is a mutual decision. The two of you should figure out what needs to be done in order to make you both comfortable.

However, do not be upset if you are the one eager to be intimate with your partner while your partner is not quite ready. Although it is true a lack of physical intimacy in a relationship that used to have thriving intimacy can be a cause for concern, the situation is different when long stretches of time physically apart are brought into the equation. This is something important that is worth committing to memory: The rules sometimes have to change when you are in a long-distance relationship.

Making the best of the time you have together

Time spent together face-to-face when you are in a long-distance relationship is incredibly precious, so consider any time you get to spend with your partner to not only be enjoyable but also something that helps strengthen your relationship. When you are in a long-distance relationship, your own life has a tendency to take over, and you might find that your concerns turn to what you need to do for work and other daily obligations as opposed to what you can do to make your relationship with your partner better. Many people fall into the trap of seemingly "forgetting" they have a partner and a relationship to be cultivated, and as a result, they put the relationship on pause until they can be together with their partners again. This leads to a scramble when together to ensure the relationship is fed instead of simply enjoying time as a couple.

For this reason, ensure you continually are feeding your relationship even when the two of you are not together, and this will make your time together face-to-face much more pleasant and worthwhile. The time and effort you put into your relationship while you are away from your partner will make the time you do have together go more smoothly. The better your relationship is overall, the better your visits are likely to be. Do not ignore the needs of your partner (and your own needs) during the stretches of time away from each other; otherwise, your visits are likely to be riddled with time spent fixing your relationship instead of spending quality time together.

This is certainly not to say you should avoid all conflict during your visit. If problems need to be discussed, discuss them. Just do not make problem-solving the focus of your visit unless it is needed and expected. This is not a time to surprise your partner with a barrage of problems; if your partner is expecting a fun, relaxing visit, there is a good chance the response to your insistence in addressing conflict will not be good.

So, what can you do during your visit to make sure you are making the most of your time together? You already know to expect some level of awkwardness and to not place unrealistic expectations on the visit. If you can enter into the visit with a realistic view of what to expect, and you are willing to keep the lines of communication open throughout the visit, then you are setting you and your partner up for a nice time together. The trick is figuring out how to balance everything without having to put too much effort into the balancing process. In other words, you do not want to be so consumed with doing everything right during the visit that you spend more time fretting than visiting. The visits you have with your partner are supposed to be enjoyable, so do not get so hung up on everything that you miss the enjoyment of the visit.

Depending on the location and duration of your visit, you might be able to schedule some fun things to do with your partner. Obviously, if the two of you have agreed to meet somewhere like Las Vegas or Hawaii, the expectation probably will be to spend some time enjoying the locale. If, on the other hand, you meet somewhere a little less exciting and touristy, you can still make solid plans for one or two fun things to do together. Even if you live in a location you otherwise would consider a relatively boring area, there is a good chance you still have a few things you can do to have some fun during your visit. Check the official tourism website for your county; you might be surprised to find a wide variety of interesting things to do around your town.

Do not forget to plan some quiet time together as well as some time to allow inspiration to hit regarding what it is the two of you want to do. If you have children, try to have some time with just you and your partner, but temper this with plenty of time for your children to have the opportunity to enjoy time with your partner as well. When you are part of a family unit, you have to keep in mind that you are not the only one who misses your partner.

Tamsen's Tip

If you are left at home with kids while your partner is away, resist the urge to consider your partner's visit to be nothing more than your break from the kids. Believe me when I say I know the urge is strong. I have planned more than one solo weekend getaway in my head when my husband was scheduled to be home temporarily. When it comes right down to it, though, I have to look at the overall benefit to my relationship with him and to my kids. Instead, I am saving a solo weekend respite for when my husband is home permanently.

You might feel that you must plan so many events during the visit or else you and your partner might not be able to click, and the entire visit will be ruined. Instead of focusing on what might happen, focus on what you hope will happen and leave some room for things to happen organically. The calmer you are, and the more peace you are with the idea that the visit might not go absolutely perfectly, the more at ease you will be with your partner and the better your chances of having a nice visit you both enjoy.

CASE STUDY: TRAVELING TO VISIT A PARTNER

Stacy, traveled across the globe with children to visit her husband

A few years ago, my husband, Eric, received military orders for a one-year remote tour at Osan Air Base in South Korea. Before this, we had spent three years stationed at Offutt Air Force Base in Nebraska, became very connected to our church and the community, and requested a follow-on to Offutt after Korea. This means that he would serve in Korea for one year and then move back to Nebraska. Because we have two young children (ages 2 and 4 at the time) and owned our home, we decided the kids and I would remain in our home in Nebraska while Eric was in Korea. To our advantage, our kids were not school age yet, so that gave us the flexibility to plan a "vacation" to go see their daddy. As we prepared for Eric to leave, we also secured passports for the kids and me in case I was actually crazy enough to fly us to the other side of the world for a visit.

After he arrived in Korea and had become a little more familiar with the culture, he was able to convince me to bring the kids out to visit him. I am still not sure how he pulled that off. Stocked with an arsenal of snacks, diapers, video games and DVDs, we were off on the adventure of a lifetime. The nearly 24 hours of travel time is a blur, but I somehow I made it, and as a bonus, I managed to do so without losing either child.

After a couple of days of adjusting to the time difference of 12 hours, we took advantage of every opportunity we could to go on tours of villages, museums, shops, fortresses, and palaces. It was amazing to experience a culture that we never would have seen otherwise. We stayed just short of a month in my husband's one bedroom dorm room on the military base. In fact, we had such a good time that Eric actually got me to agree to make the trip a second time in the following spring. Unfortunately for us, this time our travel did not go as smoothly as the first trip, but we made it nonetheless, and I still am glad that we went.

In between these two trips, Eric used his the vacation time the military provided him to come back home. By doing this, we were able to break the 12 months up so that we were able to see each other every three months. For us, this was much better than being apart for an entire year.

Although I hope we never have to have our family split apart again, I do not regret anything about that year. The experiences of our travels were amazing, and my children (who are now 5 and 8) still remember so much about the trip. The best part is that it increased my confidence as a mother. If I can travel with two small children to Korea and back — twice — then I can just about do anything.

Regardless of if your visits are frequent, or if they are quite rare, the point is to cherish the time you have together and to use this time to help strengthen the bond between the two of you. Although there is a chance that no visit ever will be perfect, you and your partner can make the mutual decision to make these visits as wonderful as is possible for the two of you. Start by deciding what is classified as "wonderful." Is a wonderful visit one spent working together on doing improvement projects around your home, or is it only wonderful if you devote a day to lounging around the house together with no agenda? Ask ten different couples what makes for the best time together, and it is likely you will get ten different responses. Figure out what works best for you, your partner, and your relationship.

Chapter 9

Avoid Being Your Own Worst Enemy

Being in a long-distance relationship can be a lonely state. You see happy couples around you, and sometimes you just want someone to help you deal with the day-to-day grind. Although today's technology allows most long-distance couples to contact each other at a moment's notice, there is no substitute for a long, warm hug from your partner at the end of a rough day. If you are not prepared to deal with the loneliness that can accompany a long-distance relationship, or if you and your partner have a difficult time keeping the lines of communication open, you might wind up sabotaging your relationship without realizing what you are doing.

Maybe being in a long-distance relationship is more difficult than anticipated, and you wonder if you should call it quits but do not want to be the one to pull the plug. Or perhaps you wound up in a long-distance relationship unintentionally and feel bitter that the person you love is miles away, and as a result, your attitude is reflective of your bitterness. Whatever the root of your angst, you need to acknowledge your feelings, figure out why you are having these feelings, and openly communicate with your partner in a way that does not place blame.

If your relationship is not going as well as you hoped, start by looking at yourself and your feelings before jumping to the conclusion that something external is causing these problems. What can you do to improve your attitude when it comes to your long-distance relationship?

The Loneliness of Long-Distance

Your need for human contact might differ from other people's depending on a variety of factors. Are you an extrovert or an introvert? Were you raised in an affectionate family? Do you find that you yearn for physical touch and feel deprived when you go long periods without being touched? The answers to these questions are different for each person, and you might find that the answers vary greatly between you and your partner. You might be the type of person who starts to feel depressed if you do not have the opportunity to hold hands and hug your partner on a regular basis, while your partner can go long periods without affectionate physical contact. Either way, keep in mind that your version of loneliness might differ greatly from everyone else's. For you, loneliness might mean a lack of physical contact. For your partner, loneliness might mean coming home to an empty house every night after work. Regardless, it is possible to be surrounded by other people yet still feel lonely. The loneliness most people feel in long-distance relationships is a loneliness stemming from a lack of intimacy — not just physical intimacy, but the emotional intimacy that comes with being one half of a couple.

Do not bury your feelings of loneliness. Instead, acknowledge your feelings, and work through them. This does not mean it is all right to wallow in your loneliness. Instead, figure out the best way to deal with your loneliness, so it does not harm your relationship. For some people, this means writing in a journal, talking with friends, or even seeing a professional therapist. The goal is to get your feelings out in a healthy way. If you keep your emotions bottled up and refuse to acknowledge them, there is a good chance your feelings are going to come out in another way, and it might not be pretty. An eruption of angry emotion, particularly when the root emotion is loneliness, is not going to do anything to make you feel better or help improve your relationship with your partner.

Tamsen's Tip

I have a few friends who also have husbands go away frequently, and we often call each other for support. These are the ladies that are willing to listen to me complain for a while, but then gently steer me back toward fixing whatever is wrong. I do the same for them. I hope you have friends like this, too.

As your long-distance relationship progresses, you will find there are ways you can learn to deal with loneliness. Many people find that it is harder to be lonely if they are engage in activities that keep them busy and engaged in socializing. For example, instead of sitting at home alone at night after dinner, go volunteer your spare time with an organization you care about or get involved with a book club that meets weekly. Schedule appointments with a personal trainer for evenings or enroll in a noncredit class at a local community college to learn something you have always wanted to learn but never seemed to have the time to do (such as photography, cooking, or another language). Do not feel guilty about engaging in these types of fun activities while you are away from your partner. A happier you will mean a happier relationship.

Always keep in mind that what works for you might not work for someone else (and vice versa), so if a friend makes a suggestion regarding a coping tactic he or she successfully used to deal with loneliness, and you find that this particular tactic does not help you, do not allow a cognitive leap to tell you there is something wrong with you or that your relationship is doomed. Acknowledge that some people deal with loneliness by spending more time with friends, and some people deal with loneliness by spending time alone doing something they enjoy. Find what works for you.

Do share your feelings of loneliness with your partner, but do not place blame or allow the emotions to culminate into something else entirely. Your partner probably will enjoy hearing, "I surely do miss you and cannot wait to see you," but probably will not enjoy hearing, "I miss you so much that I cannot function, and I cannot believe that you abandoned me like this." If you are truly so consumed with grief over the distance between the two of you that you cannot function, this is a matter to discuss with a licensed therapist. You cannot place the blame for your loneliness on the shoulders of your partner, however, because when it comes right down to it, you have the choice to remain in the relationship.

You will probably have periods when you feel lonely, and that is all right. Long-distance relationships can be stressful, so there should be no surprise when your emotions seem to get the better of you. The goal is to acknowledge that you are in the middle of a stressful situation but, eventually, there will be an end in sight (when the two of you can be together), and until then you just have to do the best you can.

Tamsen's Tip

I happen to have many friends who are men, but this does not mean that I spend a lot of one-on-one time with these men while my husband is away. I will meet with a male friend for coffee or lunch occasionally, but it is always in a public place, and it is never a secret from my husband. You will not find me going to a movie with a male friend or inviting a male friend over to my house for a private dinner while my husband is gone. I certainly could justify these things because of my loneliness in his absence, but I have to think about the perception of these events. Simply put, I do not allow my loneliness to lead me to do things that might upset my husband, thereby damaging our relationship.

In a previous chapter, you learned that you have to take care to not allow your feelings of loneliness to culminate into a situation in which you wind up getting to close to someone else. This concept is repeated here because, often, it is loneliness that drives people in long-distance relationships to seek out companionship elsewhere. Have respect for your relationship, and do not allow loneliness to justify cheating. It is counterproductive because cheating is incredibly damaging to relationships. If your goal is to flourish in your long-distance relationship, loneliness should be an emotion you acknowledge and work through instead of something that prompts events leading up to the end of your relationship.

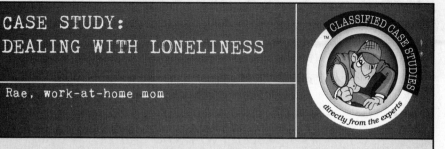

CASE STUDY:
DEALING WITH LONELINESS

Rae, work-at-home mom

My husband was deployed with the military on average six months out of the year (in one- to two-month periods) for several years. My biggest challenge — aside from the occasional major appliance that stopped working — while he was gone was finding a balance with how much I missed him. Obviously, if I spent every moment reflecting on how quiet the house was without him around, I would have been miserable the entire time he was gone. The opposite extreme of trying not to think about him so as not to miss him was not a healthy way to deal with the separation, either.

For me, the way to achieve this balance was to spend some time communicating with my husband each day about the mundane happenings of life with the both of us. In order to make this happen, we needed to be flexible with how we could communicate. Depending on his location and work schedule, sometimes it worked to have regular video chat sessions using the computer. Other times, we had to settle for daily email and the occasional phone call, but the important thing was that we had regular communication.

I do have one piece of advice for people in a similar situation. One thing I did allow myself was to be sad the first day that he left. Then, from the next day on, I would think about how as each day went by, we were one day closer to his return.

How to avoid sabotaging your relationship

Pretend that your relationship with your partner is a huge diagram featuring the cause and effect of your actions and the actions of your partner. Instead of being in the middle of all this action, you have the ability to take a step back and study the diagram on a larger scale. You can see not only where actions lead, but also what truly caused the actions in the first place. How helpful would it be to have the ability to see what each possible action would result in and to see every option for each particular decision?

You do not need a diagram to see what effect your decisions can have on your relationship with your partner. Instead, look critically at what is going on and consider what might happen if you make certain decisions. Think of it this way: Before you make a decision that possibly might sabotage your relationship, accept that you might be taking one step toward the end of your relationship.

Here is an example. Suppose you reconnect with an ex-boyfriend or ex-girlfriend online and, after revealing that your partner is away, you receive an invitation to meet for dinner at a romantic restaurant. Your ex claims that the restaurant choice is more about the food and less about the candlelight and the strolling violinist, but your ex's track record suggests there might be more to this than a simple invitation for a bite to eat. On the other hand, you remember your ex as someone who is fun to spend time with, and with your partner away, you really are craving some human interaction.

Before making your decision as to whether you will indulge in a dinner with your ex, examine some of the possible options along with what consequences those options might have. Here is a possible list:

1. **You turn down the offer for dinner, and because of your hunch about your ex's motives, you stop corresponding with him or her.** When you think about the overall health of your long-distance relationship, this is probably the best option for everyone involved. If you are trying to allow

your long-distance relationship to flourish (and not just survive), then the logical decision is not to put yourself into a potentially bad situation. If you think that going to dinner at a romantic restaurant with an ex who has ulterior motives — particularly when you are feeling deprived of human interaction — is not a bad idea, then it might be time for you to re-examine your own priorities. Are you trying to have a flourishing long-distance relationship, or are you simply trying to satisfy your own needs?

2. **You turn down dinner and, instead, suggest meeting for coffee in a public place.** This option might be a good one, but it depends on what guidelines you and your partner have set about this type of thing. Does your partner mind if you meet with an ex? A good rule of thumb is this: If you would get upset if your partner did it, you should not do it either. You also have to consider whether you will share with your partner that you are meeting with your ex. On one hand, you might be tempted to keep it a secret, even if you have absolutely no intention of doing anything wrong. Perhaps you think your partner's feelings will be hurt, or you fear your partner will be jealous if he or she knew of your plans. In instances such as this, consider that privacy is not much of luxury anymore. Suppose you meet with your ex without telling your partner, and then, that ex writes a Facebook status of "I just had coffee with (your name)," and this ex does not have privacy settings on his or her Facebook account. The next thing you know, your partner finds out online that you went to coffee with your ex. Things can get ugly quite quickly in a situation like this.

3. **You accept the offer and tell yourself nothing is going to happen, so there is no need to decline.** It was mentioned in the introduction to this hypothetical scenario that your ex's past behavior suggests he or she will probably try something with you. If you choose to ignore your intuition, you might still be hoping he or she is still attracted to you. Maybe you want some validation because you feel deprived of validation from your partner. Perhaps you want to feel as though someone finds you attractive, and you intend to rebuff any advances. Or maybe you would enjoy a tryst, and you are keeping your options open. When you think about this entire scenario critically, however, the best option for the health of your relationship is to not get yourself into this mess to begin with.

4. **You go to dinner, hoping that something will happen and assuming you can keep it secret from your partner.** As previously mentioned, privacy is not guaranteed with anything anymore. Beyond the lack of privacy, however, you need to examine the whole concept of thinking there is nothing wrong with cheating on your partner. Even if you manage to have an affair without your partner finding out, what does this mean about you and your relationship? What is wrong with your relationship that makes you think introducing deception is acceptable? If you find yourself thinking a quick affair is no big deal, you have some issues to tackle. Examine whether you are really cut out to be in long-distance relationship and, if so, if you are cut out to be in a long-distance relationship with the partner you are currently with. A long-distance relationship riddled with deceit is not going to flourish; it may continue in a mediocre state, but it will not thrive.

If you can stay true to who you are, keep the lines of communication open, and always think through the possible consequences of your actions, you give your long-distance relationship a fighting chance. In the scenario above, it was when you stopped thinking about the health of your relationship as a whole that things started to crumble. Whenever you get the urge to do something that potentially can hurt the relationship you have with your partner, stop and think about whether it is worth it. Is it worth the potential pain and embarrassment you can cause to make you feel temporarily happy or validated? You have to decide whether short-term gratification is more important than long-term gratification. After all, a long-distance relationship is all about long-term gratification. You might be frustrated because you miss your partner, but in the long term, it is worth it if you and your partner truly are meant to be together.

The goal is to have your long-distance relationship flourish, not just exist. So, if you wonder why it is so important to think everything through so thoroughly, remember that you are making important efforts to ensure your and your partner's continued happiness. Although it might take more effort to think ahead constantly as to what the consequences of your actions may be, and though it might sometimes be frustrating that you have to always take into consideration what your partner will think or feel, when it comes right down to it, the effort is worth it.

Non-exclusive long-distance relationships

Of course, the rules change if you and your partner have agreed that you will not be exclusive with each other while apart. When you and your partner are allowed to see other people, you do not have to spend as much time worrying about where your actions might lead and what the perception might be of spending one-on-one time with other people. On the other hand, just because a long-distance relationship is not exclusive, it does not mean jealousy will never arise. If your partner is upset with the time you spend with people of the opposite gender, yet the two of you do not have an exclusive relationship, you need to have a frank discussion about whether it is time for the two of you to stop seeing other people. The alternative to this is for your partner to learn how to deal with his or her jealousy issues, to accept the jealousy as inevitable, or to end the relationship. Whatever the decision is, make sure it is not fear of commitment that is keeping you both from initiating an exclusive relationship.

If your intention is to have a flourishing long-distance relationship, you might find that it is more difficult to do so when you are both allowed to date other people. How can you dedicate yourself to the growth of your relationship with your partner if you also are dedicating some of your time to romantic occurrences with others? Yes, there are some couples who manage to enjoy their long-distance relationship while also dating other people, but if your hope is to build your relationship, there is a good chance that seeing other people only will serve to stifle your long-distance relationship.

If you and your partner mutually agree to see other people while still maintaining your long-distance relationship, make all intentions clear so no one gets his or her feelings hurt. Are you allowed to sleep with other people? Are you supposed to tell your partner about your rendezvous? These questions probably will make for an awkward conversation, but knowing the clear-cut boundaries in the beginning will avoid confusion (and possibly also some anger) later on.

Trust and bitterness issues

One of the biggest obstacles people in long-distance relationships face is trust — or a lack thereof — particularly because they do not have ready access to each other as people in traditional relationships do. It is a lot more difficult to have an affair when you live with your partner and everyone around town knows you as a couple than it is to have an affair when your partner is miles away. Simply put, when you do not have ready access to your partner, you might wonder what he or she is doing when you are not around.

You have to make a decision. Are you going to trust your partner? Being in a relationship without trust involved can be a miserable arrangement. If you spend your nights fretting that your partner might be out on the town with someone else, this is not a healthy relationship. Unless your partner has given you some reason to doubt his or her commitment to you, do not waste your time with worry; no amount of fretting about what might happen is going to change the situation, nor is it going to improve your emotional state. If you are the type of person who has a tendency to worry yourself into a state of convincing yourself that the worst is happening, you will find that a long-distance relationship is a lot tougher than you thought it might be. You will have to work at not allowing your fear to consume you if you want your relationship to succeed.

Tamsen's Tip

With my husband frequently away, I had to make the decision to trust him. If I spent all of my time frantically trying to figure out his every move while away, I would drive myself crazy.

What do you do if you have a suspicion that your partner is cheating on you? It is one thing if you are the type of person who easily panics and makes unfounded assumptions, but it is another thing entirely if you generally trust your partner. Any number of things might prompt you to think something might be going on. Maybe you hear from a friend that your partner has started seeing someone else, or maybe your partner is acting distant and unavailable. Whatever the reason, if you have a solid basis for your worry, it is time to talk to your partner about your concerns.

Do not accuse your partner of cheating, but instead, tell him or her exactly what has you worried and go from there. For example, instead of saying, "I tried to call you last night, and you never picked up your phone. Tell me whom you were with," say something along the lines of, "I was frustrated when I could not get hold of you last night. It is not like you to ignore my calls, so I was worried. Why couldn't you answer my call?" The first example immediately accuses your partner of cheating and assumes that the reason the calls went unanswered was a rendezvous. The second example states what the issue was, explains why you were concerned, and then opens up the opportunity for your partner to explain what was going on.

Recognize that there probably will be times when you have a feeling that something fishy is going on, but, in reality, there is nothing going on at all. When you are away from your partner, it is incredibly easy to allow your mind to wander and to wonder whether your partner is being faithful. In most instances, particularly when your partner has never given you a reason to not trust him or her, it is best to make the decision to trust your partner. Otherwise, you probably will spend far too much time worrying about the whereabouts of your partner, and your relationship will be stifled.

It is not always so simple. You might have a feeling you cannot shake, or you might even know for sure your partner is cheating, but you are not sure how to deal with it. This is when you need to be willing to speak frankly with your partner and figure out what should happen next. You will learn more about deciding to call your relationship quits in the next chapter, but realize that a nagging feeling does not always mean that you are right, nor does a mistake made by your partner always equal the end of your relationship. You and your partner ultimately decide when your relationship ends, and for some couples, cheating is not always the end. Some couples can work through an affair, but that is a decision the two of you have to make.

Bitterness issues

Another problem many long-distance couples have to deal with is bitterness. Do any of these questions resonate as questions that have gone through your mind at some point during your relationship?

- Why does he not love me enough to find a job closer to me?

- Why did she choose her family over me?

- Why does he get to enjoy his days off over there while I stay here and take care of the kids around the clock?

- Why does everyone else get to enjoy their partner while I hardly get to see mine?

- Why did I have to have the rotten luck of falling in love with someone who cannot be here with me?

Whatever your situation, there is a good chance that at some point during your relationship, you have experienced some feelings of bitterness. Maybe your bitterness was directed at your partner or at yourself for making the decision to be in a long-distance relationship, or even to your situation in general. You might have found yourself bitter at friends in happy relationships with partners who are not long distance. Perhaps your bitterness was directed at a Valentine's Day jewelry commercial featuring a loving couple embracing because you knew that you would be spending Valentine's Day solo. Your bitterness might be fleeting, or it might be deeply ingrained in your feelings. Either way, it is important to look toward the root of your bitterness and to deal with the cause instead of allowing the bitterness to fester.

Bitterness can show up disguised as something else. Suppose you attend a dinner party where you are the only person there without a partner in attendance. The entire night you feel as though you are the oddball and have a miserable time. You spend the entire drive home feeling frustrated by your experience. When you get home, you call your partner and release a tirade of all the things that bother you about being in a long-distance relationship, but fail to mention that you had just come from a dinner party where you felt like a fifth wheel. All your partner knows is that you are on the attack, but if you had analyzed your feelings beforehand, it probably would be obvious that you are not bitter about your long-distance relationship. Instead, you are bitter about one night and the frustration you felt from being alone at the party where everyone else had a partner. The more your frustration festered, the bitterer you felt. By the time you got home and got the phone in your hand, you were ready to unleash a tirade on your unsuspecting partner.

Tamsen's Tip

I do get tired of attending functions without my husband, so occasionally, I will bring a friend along, so I do not have to go solo. It is amazing how much more fun a dinner party or other event can be.

You cannot spend all of your time wallowing in bitterness and still hope to have a flourishing long-distance relationship. It comes down to your decision to stay in your long-distance relationship. Every day you remain in your long-distance relationship should be considered a triumph and one day closer to seeing your partner again — not a day that was horrible because of your partner's physical absence. You have the choice either to be bitter about your circumstances or to instead make the best of it by remembering that someone out there cares enough about you to be willing to be in a relationship with you. Many people cannot make that claim; make the best of what you have, and think about how strong your relationship will be when the two of you no longer have to maintain your relationship from a distance. Successfully maintaining a long-distance relationship is not only something to be proud of, but it is also something that helps prove the dedication you and your partner have for each other.

Tamsen's Tip

When my husband was overseas for a year in Honduras, I had a hard time dealing with hearing about all the fun he was having while I was stateside with the kids. He enjoyed sleeping in on weekends, evenings to himself, and at one point enthusiastically told me about a zipline adventure he had enjoyed in the jungle. I examined my emotions and realized I was not bitter about him having fun but was exhausted from the rigors of taking care of everything back home on my own. If I had allowed bitterness to take over, I might have demanded he stop having fun, which would have not been a good solution, of course.

The next time you feel bitter about your long-distance relationship, take the time to examine what you are feeling and pinpoint the cause of your emotion. Are you bitter because your partner gets to sleep in on Saturdays while you attend to children (or whatever the imbalance might be), or are you in a situation where you need to learn to control your jealousy of your partner's free time? Your emotions are a choice; you can choose whether you are going to allow negative feelings to take over or if you will try to deal with your emotions as logically as possible.

Dealing with Danger

It is one thing to worry that your partner might get hit by a bus while crossing a busy intersection or contract a serious illness, but it is another thing entirely when your partner is in a situation in which there is a valid concern for his or her well-being. Partners who are stationed in a military combat zone, who are incarcerated, or who have jobs that innately feature some element of danger, can increase the stress levels associated with a long-distance relationship exponentially. Not only do you miss your partner, but you also constantly worry about your partner's safety.

For most long-distance couples, a delay in communication is not anything to be alarmed by, but when your partner is in potential danger, communication delays can start your mind reeling. Did he not call because he is injured? Is the reason I did not receive a letter this week is that she is lying in a hospital bed? Did he not return my email message because he died last night? It is easy to allow your mind to fast-forward toward the worst-case scenario when your partner is in a dangerous situation. If you remember the concept mentioned earlier of "cognitive leaps," you already know your mind can create some wild assumptions from the littlest things and work you into an emotional state of sheer panic from something as simple as a missed phone call.

Here is one of the most important things to remember when it comes to having a partner in a dangerous situation: No amount of worry is going to change the circumstances. Whether you stay awake at night in fear that your partner is hurt, or if you sleep soundly through the night, whatever is going to happen is going to happen. Refusing to allow yourself to get worked into a frenzy about things you cannot change is a defense mechanism that can help you get through this tough time. When you indulge in constant panic, you are harming your physical well-being, as your immune system wears down from lack of sleep and increased stress hormones. Instead, use coping mechanisms to help you deal with the stress, so you can stay healthy while awaiting your partner's return.

Here are some suggestions for dealing with your partner being in a dangerous situation:

- Stop watching the news if your partner is in a combat situation. Although it is generally good to be informed, watching video clips of explosions and civil unrest only is going to panic you. Remember: Not all military people deployed overseas are involved in combat. Your partner might spend more time behind a desk in an air-conditioned office than wandering through the streets of a combat zone.

- Decide whether you are going to tell people your partner's whereabouts. You might have a good grip on dealing with your partner's dangerous situation, but other people might not. In other words, if you tell someone at a dinner party that your partner is currently a trucker navigating the dangerous, icy roads of Alaska, the horrified look you receive might be enough to put you into an internal panic. You might start to doubt your own confidence in your partner's eventual return. If you are going to tell people about your partner's dangerous occupation or situation, prepare yourself beforehand to shrug off any reactions that otherwise would make you panic.

- Find someone to talk with about your feelings. You do not want to bottle up your fear, nor do you want to disregard it only to have it sneak up on you later and explode. A therapist or clergyperson who is well versed in dealing with long-distance couples is the best option, but a friend who is willing to listen and not allow you to go overboard with your panic is a good alternative if you do not have any other options available to you. If you do not feel comfortable talking about your feelings, journal your feelings on a regular basis.

Tamsen's Tip

If your partner is away on a military assignment, check with the local military installation to find out what resources are available to you. Counseling, free babysitting, and even car care are just a few of the resources offered to military families with a deployed member.

- Having a strong spiritual belief system can be a huge help during your partner's absence, but this is especially true when your partner is in a dangerous situation. Whether you pray, meditate, or simply give your worries over to God, it can help to know that there is a bigger plan than what you can see. Trusting in a higher power to keep your partner safe (and to keep you calm during this stressful time) can provide you with a great deal of comfort.

- Consider trying out some calming physical activities, such as yoga, Tai chi, or leisurely walks through nature. What is it you do that makes you feel calm and at peace? Include regular exercise in your normal routine, but also make time for physical activity that helps you feel at ease regardless of the stress you are under.

- Pay attention to how the people in your life react to your situation, and spend less time with toxic people. Do you have a cubicle neighbor who winces every time you mention your partner's location? Do you have a family member who makes passive-aggressive comments about your partner's safety? If you cannot get the toxic people in your life to stop sending harmful jabs your way, then make the decision that now is not the right time to have these people in your life.

- Remember that your partner might be scared, too. If you have never been in a dangerous situation, you cannot pretend to know how your partner feels. Instead of unloading your emotions on your partner, lamenting about how hard this is on *you*, tell your partner that you are scared but you know this is not a permanent situation. It might help if you tell your partner that you are praying for him or her, sending good thoughts his or her way, or however you want to phrase it to let him or her know that you care and are genuinely concerned. For many people in dangerous situations, it helps tremendously to know that someone back home is thinking about them.

If you are the partner who is in harm's way, you might be inclined either to censor everything about what you are experiencing, or instead, you might have the desire to give your partner every panicked detail about what you deal with on a day-to-day basis. Instead, try to find a delicate balance that allows you to share your experiences with your partner while only giving your partner as much as he or she can effectively deal with. Stories of near-death experiences, wild confrontations, or moments when you did not know if you would make it out alive perhaps are best shared with your partner once you are safely back home — or not shared at all if you know that your life will put you back into a similar situation in the future. Do you really want your partner obsessing about the story of how you almost died while deployed if you are going to deploy again? You have to decide what you think your partner can handle.

This is certainly not to say you should censor your entire life from your partner, because this is not an effective method of communication between two people in a committed long-distance relationship. Instead, it is important to remember that tales of your near-demise might be better suited for another time as opposed to revealing these events to your partner over the phone when you still have a couple more months before you return home. This is a decision you have to make; you know your partner, and you know what your partner can handle.

When something happens

What happens if something bad actually does happen to your partner while he or she is away? If your partner gets injured, you might feel frantic about trying to find a way to help him or her. In instances when it is not feasible for you to rush to your partner's bedside (such as with a military deployment overseas in a combat area or when you do not have the money to hop on a plane), it can be a huge challenge to try to stay calm.

Try to acknowledge what you can do and what you cannot do. You can pray for your partner, you might be able to talk to him or her on the phone, and you can pull together a get-well care package to send through the mail. You can provide as much moral support as possible and can rally mutual friends to do the same. What you cannot do is change the past. You are probably not in a position to help your partner physically heal unless he or she is able to return to your home to recover. Do not despair in the things you cannot do for your injured partner, but instead turn your efforts toward the things that you can do to try to help.

You might find yourself in a situation when your partner's injuries are severe enough to change the way he or she lives. Suppose your partner returned from a military deployment with the inability to walk. Or what if your partner's dramatic fall and head injury during a mountain climbing expedition resulted in limited cognitive functioning? What if a car accident left your partner with so much emotional trauma that he or she becomes unable to ride in a vehicle without experiencing debilitating anxiety? In instances such as these, in which physical injuries have the potential to change fundamentally the way a person lives, you have a job as the person's partner to try to help where you can while also being realistic about what you can handle.

An injury to your partner impacts you. Turn to your trusted friends and family for support, and do not dwell on what-ifs. Do not allow yourself to feel guilty if you try to do things to cheer yourself up while dealing with having a partner who is away and injured. No one should criticize you for going out to dinner with a friend or going to a funny movie while your partner recovers from his or her injuries miles away. Anyone who gives you grief about your attempts to lighten your mood during this stressful time does not understand the massive amounts of stress you are going through.

If possible, speak with a trained counselor who has experience helping people in similar situations. You might not understand all of the emotions you are feeling during this extraordinarily stressful time, and someone who is well versed in helping people work through these situations will prove to be invaluable.

Dealing with other stressors

There is no predicting what can happen when your partner is away. You might have to deal with a death in the family, an unexpected job loss that results in a huge shift in your financial standing, or a natural disaster that displaces you from your home. Many people deal better with these unexpected life events when they have a partner who is there to support them, but when your partner is away and cannot be at your side to help you through the tough times, you might find yourself feeling overwhelmed.

Tamsen's Tip

My grandmother passed away when my husband was overseas on a military assignment. I really could have used his physical presence at that time, but he still tried to be as supportive as possible from a distance. His being a listening ear was the best thing he could do for me at that time, and it was a great deal of help to me when dealing with my grief.

If you are the partner who is dealing directly with the unexpected stressful event, try to keep the lines of communication open with your partner as much as possible. The more you put on a happy face and hide how you really feel about the situation, the less your partner will understand what you are going through. Share your feelings with your partner, and give your partner the opportunity to comfort you even if the comfort has to come in the form of a telephone conversation or email correspondence. Avoid the temptation to allow your grief to turn into something else; grief is a powerful emotion, and if you are not careful, you might find a conversation that began about the stressful event quickly evolves into a conversation about how you do not know if you can handle being in a long-distance relationship anymore. When discussing your grief with your partner, focus on the topic at hand, and tell your partner how you feel. If you try to mask the emotion, it might come out as something else.

If you are the partner who is away and are trying to comfort your partner from afar, do not be surprised if you feel a great deal of frustration when dealing with this issue. You might feel guilt because you do not have to deal with the problem directly, and you might feel helpless because you cannot be there to comfort your partner. You also might wonder if you will say the wrong thing, or if you will not be able to find the right words to comfort your partner. Try to focus less on saying everything perfectly, and, instead, focus on letting your partner know you are willing to listen and to help in any way possible. Give your partner a little grace at this time, too; if your partner has a little less patience with you, taking it personally is not going to help anything. If your partner just experienced the death of a family member, was just laid off unexpectedly from work, or had to evacuate his or her home to avoid a major storm, this is not the time to expect cheerfulness from your partner. Acknowledge that your partner is experiencing high stress levels and might be less than cordial. This does not give your partner a free pass to berate you or say horrible things that are going to leave a lasting impact. Instead, it means your partner might be distracted, short with words, or not even want to talk.

The best thing you can do if your partner is going through a tough time is to try to be as supportive as possible in whatever way you can. This might mean staying up late talking to your partner on the phone while he or she cries. It also might mean accepting that it is not time to talk about your day, and the small inconveniences you experienced (imagine your partner listening to you complaining about getting cut off in traffic when your partner just lost his or her house.). You have to decide what topics are appropriate based on what your partner needs at the time. Maybe your partner does want you to talk about your day because this makes him or her feel more "normal" in a chaotic time. Read your partner's cues and decide what is appropriate for the time being.

This is also not a time to cling tightly to the purse strings. If you and your partner share expenses, and your partner's unexpected stressful event incurs some extra costs, this is not something to complain about. For example, suppose you and your partner diligently have been saving money so you can visit each other the upcoming Christmas season. Your partner's uncle dies unexpectedly, and your partner wants to use the money you have both been saving for your visit to attend her uncle's funeral. Before automatically complaining about how this money was earmarked for another purpose, think about how you would feel if it was your uncle. Also, think about the lasting implications of the decision you make; your partner might consider your complaints a direct result of your selfishness. This is not to say you are actually selfish, but remember that grief can have a peculiar way of changing a person's perspective. Try to put yourself in your partner's shoes, and try to be as patient as possible. What you might not realize is that your partner is not only dealing with the stressful event but is also having to deal with the stressful event without your presence.

Chapter 10

Knowing When to Call It Quits

Your relationship might last forever. Your partner might be your one true love, and you both might enjoy a long, happy life together filled with laughter and love.

On the other hand, your relationship might end.

Not all relationships make it, and when you add the extra stressor of being in a relationship long distance, the odds of staying together might decrease. After all, maintaining a long-distance relationship can be quite difficult, particularly if you want to end every evening snuggling, if you have a wandering eye, or if your partner needs constant (and relentless) reassurance of a solid relationship. Although these things do not doom your long-distance relationship, they certainly can be factors that will make it even harder to stay together.

So, what happens when you start to get the nagging feeling that your relationship is not working? Although other couples might have the opportunity to march into a counselor's office and work through their issues, when you are in a long-distance relationship, you do not have this luxury. With all the added factors that can come with a long-distance relationship (sporadic communication, awkwardness when together, opportunities to keep things from each other), trying to work through problems from a distance can prove to be incredibly difficult. How do you know when it is worth it to stay together? How do you know when to throw your hands up in resignation and walk away from the relationship and when to buckle down and do whatever you have to do to stay together? The answer depends on your relationship and what issues are making you question the commitment.

There is a big difference between ending a month-long relationship with someone you met online and ending a ten-year marriage that resulted in a mortgage, three kids, and a shared small business. Although both relationships have the potential to hurt when they end, one has more of a lasting affect than the other when it comes to the damage that can be done. If you break up with your month-long online partner, you likely will be able to chalk up the whole relationship to a lesson learned and move on with your life. On the other hand, if you break up with your spouse, you are disrupting the lives of your children, changing the anticipated course of your life, and potentially causing financial heartache for you, your partner, or both of you. Although you should not take the end of any relationship lightly, ending a long-term relationship should be considered an important decision with long-lasting repercussions.

Signs of Trouble

When you think you see signs of trouble in your long-distance relationship, first examine everything to make sure what you are experiencing is not the result of assumptions and cognitive leaps on your part. Is there really a problem, or have you assumed there is a problem because things are not going the way you thought (or hoped) they would?

Not all problems equal the end of a relationship. Long-distance or not, some couples fight to stay together despite problems and wind up in incredibly strong relationships as a result. It is up to you to decide what your threshold for problems is; what is the absolute, drop-dead thing you will not tolerate, no matter what? Will you leave if your partner cheats on you? Is the relationship over if your partner is abusive? Is the relationship doomed if your partner does not call you every night at 7 p.m. sharp? Be reasonable in your demands upon your partner, but also keep your best interests in mind. Although it might not be reasonable for your partner to call you every single night at the exact same time, it is completely reasonable for you to demand safety and security from your partner.

The following list of trouble signs is not exhaustive, but it is also not absolute. There might be things you are willing to accept that are on this list, and things you will not accept that are not. The list is meant to be a starting point to help you figure out if your relationship is heading downhill. Remember that a struggling relationship might be salvageable, but it is up to you and your partner to decide if you want to put forth the effort or move on with your lives.

The trouble list

- Does your partner seem to be one person while away, but another person when you are physically together? If a dislike for communicating with phones and computers is not to blame for the awkwardness, this might be a sign that you are not getting the real version during visits.

- Does your partner belittle you or make you feel threatened? A partner who demoralizes you is not a partner — he or she is a tyrant.

- Has your partner cheated on you, or do you feel you are being cheated on? *This was discussed in Chapter 9 and will be discussed more in this chapter.* You have to decide if a cheating partner is a partner worth keeping.

- Does your partner make unrealistic demands on you or your time? This might be a sign that your partner is insecure in your relationship; it may be a sign that you have not set boundaries sufficiently, or it may be a sign that your partner is selfish.

- Does your partner not have time for you? Long-distance relationships take a lot of effort and need extra attention. If your partner (or you) does not have the time (or desire) to put toward the relationship, how can you expect it to flourish?

- Do you find yourself thinking about other people in a romantic way, and you think you might like to act upon these feelings? This can be a sign of bigger problems within your relationship and is something you should sort out instead of resorting to infidelity.

- Do you find your partner an annoyance? If you roll your eyes when your partner calls, or if you sigh heavily when email from your partner shows up in your inbox, consider this a tangible sign of problems.

- Have you discovered that you and your partner have two drastically different versions of what your future together looks like? If you are not on the same page, or do not think you will be on the same page anytime soon, it is incredibly hard for your relationship to flourish.

- Are you unhappy? Problems with your relationship can culminate into a general feeling of unhappiness in your life that you cannot really pinpoint. If you have a general sadness in life, examine your relationship, and see if it is the root cause of your unhappiness.

- Is there no end in sight to your long-distance relationship? A partner who is unwilling to move to be with you (or you not willing to move to be with your partner) shows an unwillingness to make the relationship work altogether.

- Are you just not cut out to be in a long-distance relationship? You might love your partner, but for some people, the stress that accompanies a long-distance relationship is just too much to deal with.

Did any of the above ring true for you? Note that nearly all of the items in the list above are things that can be acknowledged and worked through, especially when both partners are willing to work through anything to keep the relationship together. A lot depends on your own willingness to fix whatever the problem is, the willingness of your partner to do the same, and the limitations you have set for what you are willing to accept. You might love your partner dearly, but if you refuse to accept cheating or abuse and either of those things occur, that likely will be the end of the relationship, and for good reason. Although it can be wonderful to be in a relationship with someone you love, it is more important to truly love yourself and have enough respect for yourself to set clear boundaries. A person who truly loves you will not set out to harm you.

A no-fault ending

As painful as it may be, there might come a point in your long-distance relationship where it is no longer feasible to be together. Suppose you met your partner in another country while on vacation, or you both have your own respective reasons why you cannot move from where you live. Although the two of you put a lot of effort into making it work long distance, and you have genuine affection for one another, the realization hits that there is no way ever to be together physically. Despite the feelings you have for each other, you mutually agree that the time has come to part ways.

If this is the case, allow yourself to grieve the loss of the relationship. Part as friends instead of allowing the frustration of the situation to culminate into a massive quarrel that leaves the both of you hurt. Some people have the tendency to pick fights and distance themselves from their long-distance partners when they have the realization that the relationship has to end. It is as if ending on bad terms makes it an easier breakup because there is no painful discussion about feelings. The truth is that you can never know what the future might bring, and there might come a time when the two of you can be together. Ending the relationship cordially leaves that option open and allows you to feel as though the relationship was fulfilling while it lasted. Ending the relationship with a screaming match (and masking your real feelings) only does damage.

Tamsen's Tip

Do not allow a relationship to end based on an involuntary presumption of "I can't." Instead of automatically presuming, "I cannot move to another country!" or "I cannot sell my business and move," consider that maybe you can actually do these things.

Infidelity

Cheating happens, and when a relationship is long-distance, cheating can become easier to pull off without getting caught. Some people get so starved for physical touch that they seemingly cannot help but to wind up in a situation where they are cheating, and others get into affairs because they do not feel emotionally satisfied in their long-distance relationship. No matter what the excuse, cheating is a decision that is made.

That is an important point to keep in mind about cheating when in a long-distance relationship: It is a decision. When you cheat on your partner, you make the decision to disrespect your partner. You break promises and make a mockery of your commitment. If your partner cheats on you, what your partner is effectively saying to you is, "I know I said I would not cheat on you, but for a brief moment, I decided it was worth it. I cannot be trusted."

Some couples can work through cheating, but you have to decide if it is worth it. A long-distance relationship that has experienced infidelity is going to be a difficult relationship to maintain, let alone hope to flourish. Consider how difficult it can be not to talk to your partner whenever you want, and then consider how much more difficult it would be if you had to worry that the reason you cannot reach your partner is because he or she is with someone else. The pain that comes with being cheated on can be significant, and it damages the relationship to a point where things probably will never be the same.

Even if you forgive your partner — or if your partner forgives you — there always will be the thought in the back of your mind that something is going on. Trust is hard to regain after an infidelity situation because it is now a tangible worry that your partner might cheat *again*. That can be an incredibly powerful motivator to make you worry incessantly, and a long-distance relationship fraught with worry is not going to be a strong, vibrant relationship.

There are different versions of infidelity. A kiss is different from a weekend-long tryst in a hotel room. You have to decide if what you or your partner has done is enough to end the relationship. Make this a definitive decision and be honest about your motivation. If your partner cheated on you, and this is why you are ending the relationship, explain why the relationship is over, and then end it. Do not linger in the relationship, knowing in your heart that you cannot ever get over the betrayal.

On the flip side, if your partner cheated on you, and you decided to stay because you have forgiven him or her, truly forgive and work on making the relationship better instead of throwing the affair into your partner's face every time the two of you have an argument. If you know that you cannot get over the affair, you should not be in the relationship. If you are the person who cheated and your partner has forgiven you, commit to making the cheating a one-time mistake. If you start to feel the urge to cheat again, take a close look at whether you should be in this relationship. How can you hope to allow your long-distance relationship to flourish if you keep indulging in betrayal?

Emotional affairs

Whereas physical affairs are conscious decisions (your clothes do not simply fall off, after all), an emotional affair can sneak up on you. It might start as a friendship you start to rely on when your partner is away, and you slowly start to realize you look forward to seeing your friend more than you should. You start to share intimate emotional moments with this friend, telling him or her about how difficult it is for you to be away from your partner. Perhaps you start to care about your appearance more when you know you will see this friend. Maybe you have butterflies in your stomach when the two of you are together. The next thing you know, you are admitting to your friend that you are attracted to him or her (or vice versa), but you both agree nothing physical will ever happen between you.

Is this an affair? Even if there is no physical contact between you and your friend beyond an occasional hug or quick kiss on the cheek, many people will still consider this an affair for a few reasons. An intimacy is created that should be reserved for a partner, not a friend. The two people acknowledge that romantic feelings exist, and when this happens, a decision has to be made. Simply put, your long-distance relationship is not going to flourish if you are emotionally involved with someone else. You cannot maintain both relationships without someone eventually getting hurt, whether that is your partner, your friend, or you.

Emotional affairs also can lead to physical affairs if they are not stopped before it is too late. You might find yourself involved with someone who truly cares about you, or it might be an instance of a friend taking advantage of you during your partner's absence. Either way, if you truly want to pursue a relationship with your friend, first end things with your long-distance partner. It is far better to break things off with your partner before you do something as fundamentally damaging as having an affair.

If you are unsure as to whether you are having an emotional affair with your friend, ask yourself this question: If your partner could listen in on the conversations you have with your friend (or read the email you exchange), what would your partner's reaction be? You also might wonder how you would feel if you were able to listen in on a conversation between your partner and a friend, and if the conversation was similar to conversations you have with your friend, how would you feel? Would you feel as if you were being cheated on?

Chances are good that you will flirt, but whether that flirting becomes something else is another matter entirely. When you start doing things your partner would consider wrong, or if your partner starts doing things you would consider wrong, you have to wonder what you are doing maintaining your long-distance relationship in the first place. Staying in your relationship is a choice; why choose to be in a relationship that is not fulfilling you? If you want to be with your friend, be with your friend. If you want to be with your partner, be with your partner. Just do whatever you choose wholeheartedly.

Problems are Normal

Your long-distance relationship is not going to be perfect. You will encounter problems that need to be solved, make mistakes that need to be forgiven, and have times when you wonder if the relationship is really worth all the effort you have to put into it to make it work. Every relationship has problems to overcome, and the trick is to realize that problems do not necessarily guarantee your relationship is not going to work.

Think of problems in your relationship as opportunities to resolve something and come out with an even stronger relationship than what you had before the problem. In fact, if you are involved in a long-distance relationship in which your partner never disagrees with you and never has a bad thing to say about anything, you might want to wonder whether your partner is presenting an accurate representation of him or herself. It is much easier to pretend to be someone you are not when you see your partner infrequently, particularly when you have no mutual friends. Consider a complete lack of conflict to be a sign of a much bigger problem than having problems occasionally that wind up resolved.

How you and your partner react to problems can have a huge impact on the strength of your relationship. Suppose you have an argument with your partner over the phone, and you are so frustrated that you need some time to cool down before you can further the discussion in a reasonable way. Instead of abruptly hanging up on your partner and explaining your actions later, explain to your partner right then that you need some time to calm down and will call back soon. Your partner should respect this and give you the time you need, just as you should respect the situation and not allow a great deal of time to pass before you call back to resolve the issues. If you and your partner can have respectful conversations — even when disagreeing — your relationship will not be impacted negatively when you do disagree.

Even big issues can be resolved if you and your partner are willing to work together and be patient. This is where being in a long-distance relationship might be to your benefit. If you are so angry at your partner for something that coming home to him or her only would result in a heated argument, you can be glad that your partner is away, and you have the time you need to think things through.

When you have problems in your long-distance relationship, examine what the root cause of the issue is, and then, keep the lines of communication open with your partner in order to work through the problem together. Do not assume the presence of problems means your relationship cannot work or that you are not cut out for being in a long-distance relationship. Instead of giving up, try to work through the problems and see if you can make your long-distance relationship work.

```
CASE STUDY:
EXPERT ADVICE

Reverend Michael Moore
```

CLASSIFIED CASE STUDIES
™
directly from the experts

Long-distance relationships can be a great challenge and an incredible blessing at the same time. The blessing is that the couple comes to appreciate and value time spent together because it is so precious and rare. However, the flip side of that blessing is that the couple can do one of two things: either ignore or gloss over issues in the relationship because "we do not want to waste our time together focusing on the negative," or only do the fun things because they do not have enough time for depth. The key to maintaining and strengthening the relationship is good communication.

Communication limited to emails and texts (and even written letters) is not always the best because so much can be lost in translation. Non-verbal cues, tone of voice — these are crucial if the communication is to be whole. A text or written word might be misunderstood because you are reading them without the benefit of hearing and/or seeing the individual communicating. Phone conversations play a big role in keeping those lines of communication open and with videoconference tools like Skype, you can talk and see the individual. That can alleviate so much misunderstanding in these long-distance relationships.

Another key to communication is what the experts call "active listening." This can seem, at first, sort of artificial or staged, but as the tool is used, it becomes natural and effective. Especially when a couple is in disagreement, this tool helps you truly hear what the other person is saying instead of thinking up the snappy retort or zinger to show the other that you are in the right, and they are obviously in the wrong. How do you hear what they are saying? After they speak (one marital counseling tool calls this "having the floor"), the listener has to respond back with a phrase such as "I hear you saying…" and then paraphrasing what they said. The speaker (holding the floor), has the opportunity to either affirm that the listener heard correctly or to respond in a non-judgmental way with what they were meaning the other to hear. This is effective over the phone, in person, and via Skype.

So, how does a couple make the decision either to call it quits on such a relationship or seek help? There are some signals common to all couples in addition to signals that are unique to each relationship. There is not a cookie-cutter approach or answer to this question. The following guidelines and observations are gleaned from years of practical and personal experience.

Has the relationship fallen into a rut or an unhealthy pattern? Are you arguing continuously about finances? About time management? About relationships with others? Are you looking for excuses to avoid spending time with your partner? Are your letters, emails, or phone calls negative or whiny? Do you have a hard time remembering the last good conversation or experience you had together? Are you, in the words of the country song, "looking for love in all the wrong places" by seeking companionship that is more than friendship with others because you believe something is missing from your relationship? Are you hiding things or people from your partner? These questions indicate significant problems in the relationship that need to be addressed quickly.

There is not a "passing" or "failing" score with these questions. However, if you were to sit down, write a positive and negative list about the relationship ("What I love about him/her" and "What bothers me about him/her"), and come up with more negative than positive, there is a problem. Before calling it quits or throwing in the towel: Often, if a couple humbly and honestly admits there are problems and is willing to talk about them with a neutral third party, it can be the first step toward reconciliation. If reconciliation does not happen, it will not be for a lack of effort. How do you counsel when there is distance involved? It can be done in several ways. In my career with the Air Force, I sometimes would "tag-team" with a chaplain at another military installation to team counsel the couple. We used the same marital counseling inventory as a foundation to work from and would communicate between counselors via email or telephone. These efforts would help prepare the couple for both face-to-face counseling with one of the chaplains and for their own time spent together. Counseling also can be done with the couple and one counselor via video-teleconference or Skype. That way, the counselor and the couple cannot only hear what is being said but also read the non-verbal cues.

Chapter 11

Games and Quick Tips

You have the most important things you need to know about keeping your long-distance relationship strong and flourishing: open communication, trust, and a mutual respect. Now it is time to have some fun.

You do not have to limit your communication to talking about your future, discussing your emotions, or working through issues. Make time for fun between you and your partner even when you are separated by distance. The silliest of games or the briefest of notes can bring the two of you closer together. You want your partner to know he or she is on your mind, even when you cannot be there to say so in person.

You might be the type of person who can think of a wide variety of ways to stay connected with your partner from a distance, but if you are the type of person who needs a little help to figure out games and other quick ways to remind your partner that he or she is on your mind, use the following ideas to help you get started.

Long-Distance Games

There never has been a better time to be in a long-distance relationship when it comes to staying in touch through games. As long as you and your partner both have access to a computer and the Internet, there is a huge selection of games to choose from. Whether you want to assume a virtual life where you "visit" your partner in a world you create together, or if you prefer to play more traditional games like chess, there are plenty of options to choose from. Talk to your partner about what he or she prefers, and try several available games before deciding on favorites for the two of you.

You might be cringing at the thought of sitting down in front of a computer screen and delving into virtual worlds, even if it means spending virtual time with your partner. If online gaming gives you the image in your mind of socially deprived people staring blankly at computer screens, keep in mind you have the opportunity to try out several games before deciding on one over the other. Remember that you are not necessarily using the game as a form or mindless entertainment (although, if that is what you are looking for, this can be an added bonus), but instead, you are using it as a tool to stay connected to your partner when the two of you cannot be physically together. You should not feel guilty about the time you spend playing games with your partner any more than you should feel guilty sitting down to write a letter to your partner; you are using the games as a way to stay connected.

Tamsen's Tip

Be careful with online gaming. Use it to connect to your partner, but do not use it as an escape from the stresses of life. If you find yourself staying up after your normal bedtime to finish a virtual mission or skipping out on social activity to spend time gaming, you might be developing a gaming problem. Monitor your usage and use it primarily as a way to spend time with your partner.

Conquering the virtual world hand in hand

If you never have delved into the world of online gaming, get ready to be amazed at all the options available to you. There are some games in which you can create a character and live a virtual life, building a home, falling in love with other characters (played by other people), and being anything you want it to be. An example of this type of game is Sims™, a great option for couples that are apart and want to "meet up" virtually. Create your character, build your home, decide on a job, and socialize with other people in the virtual world.

Games like Sims are perfect for couples that are apart. You both create your characters and then agree on what time to log on and meet up. The two of you can then go on virtual dates, which can be anything from eating dinner together to shopping to strolling through a park. This can be good particularly for couples who do not have ready access to calling on the phone but who do have access to the Internet. It is also a good option for people who do not particularly enjoy talking on the phone or who prefer to meet online because they enjoy the format of the meeting.

On the other hand, if you do not particularly care for computer games, you might be resistant to participating in this type of on-line activity. If it is something your partner wants to try, or if you do not feel as though the communication between the two of you has been everything it should be, it is at least worth a shot. Try it, and if you do not like it, then at least, you can say you tried. You might find that you look forward to your virtual dates; it might not be time physically spent together, but it is better than nothing.

Perhaps you or your partner want something a little more exciting than strolling through a virtual park together. Games like World of Warcraft allow you to not only create a character and socialize with other characters created by other people, but also to go out on virtual missions in mythical lands. This means you and your partner can meet in a virtual world and then set off together to defeat evil creatures. This can be a lot of fun for couples that enjoy online gaming, and it can serve as time together even though the two of you are miles apart.

If none of the above options appeal to you, there are many other games to choose from that have nothing to do with creating a virtual character. If you and your partner enjoy games of chess, card games, or just about any other game, look for options online that will allow you to play with your partner in real time. The point is to find something that can bring you and your partner together to do something you both enjoy.

Offline games

Maybe you or your partner does not have reliable access to the Internet, or perhaps the thought of sitting in front of a computer screen playing games does not appeal to you in the least. Many options are still available to you using other forms of communication.

Get creative about the games you play together. For example, play a game of checkers together by snapping pictures of the checkers board after your move, and then waiting for your partner's next move to be sent to you in a photo. This is a great option if you have a cell phone with picture-taking capabilities or even as something you do through the mail if that is your only option. The point is not necessarily to win the game but, instead, is to have something that the two of you are doing together even though you are miles apart from each other. It might seem silly to drag a game of checkers out for days (or weeks, or months), but think about what the checker board sitting on your table will remind you of — you and your partner are willing to connect with each other and work toward staying connected even though you are apart.

You do not have to limit your games to checkers. Consider Monopoly, dominoes, or whatever game the two of you both enjoy, and get creative about how you play together. The more special you can make your game time together, the more meaningful the experience will be for the both of you.

Think outside the box

Having a private game between you and your partner can be another way to stay connected. For example, set up a game between you and your partner in which every time you Skype, your partner has to guess where you have hidden an item behind you or maybe has to guess where you are Skyping from. Create a decoder your partner has to use to decode messages you hide within your emails or letters. Send trivia questions to one another based on your favorite movies or books. Send a stuffed animal back and forth through the mail that you take turns drawing on, adding ridiculous decorations, or whatever else you want to do to keep the joke going. You and your partner should decide what will work for the two of you.

Do not underestimate the effect these silly things can have on your relationship. Your partner most likely will appreciate that you are willing to take the time to stay connected, even if the things the two of you are doing are as silly as playing a three-month-long game of checkers or slowly mangling a stuffed bear over a period of several weeks. The point is to do these things together.

If the two of you are able to watch your favorite shows together via Skype or over the phone, consider adding games to that. If you are both of legal drinking age, add a fun drinking game to the show; every time a person on the show says a certain word you decided upon beforehand, you each take a drink. This is only one example of how you can make your time spent together (while apart) even more special.

You and your partner might be able to devise something else entirely to keep you connected using games. These games help the two of you still manage to enjoy time spent together, which can be difficult when you cannot be together physically. The effort is certainly worth it, though, because time spent laughing together is time well spent.

Quick Tips

Not every effort to let your partner know you are thinking about him or her involves a great deal of preplanning or ongoing participation between the two of you. Sometimes all it takes is a quick, simple effort to remind your partner he or she is on your mind. The goal is not to just let your long-distance relationship survive, but to thrive.

Make an effort to work your way through this checklist of tips before you see your partner again:

- ❑ Change your Facebook or Twitter status to say you miss your partner, tagging him or her in your post.

- ❑ Send your partner a postcard from a place you like to visit together.

- ❑ Call your partner when you know voice mail will pick up, and leave a sweet message.

- ❑ Call the radio station near your partner, and dedicate a song to him or her.

- ❑ Send flowers or candy to your partner for no reason.

- ❑ Create a CD with your favorite songs, and send it to your partner. Take it a step further by adding a photo montage.

- ❑ Create a website with a countdown clock of when the two of you will see each other again.

- ❑ Order a pizza or other takeout to be delivered to your partner's home as a surprise.

- ❑ Create a short film featuring places your partner likes to visit, and send it to him or her.

- ❑ Send a text that says, "I miss you."

- ❑ Mail an unexpected gift to your partner.

❑ Arrange for a massage or other relaxing treat for your partner in his or her town.

❑ Write a love letter to your partner.

❑ Do something in honor of your partner, like running a 5K or donating money to charity.

❑ Plan a fun day for your partner from afar by sending gift cards for a local movie theater, museum, restaurant, or elsewhere close to your partner. You probably can purchase these cards online or over the phone.

❑ Send your partner a bottle of your perfume or cologne, so he or she can enjoy your scent in your absence.

❑ Send a copy of a book to your partner, and keep a copy for yourself, so you can read the book together.

❑ Snap pictures of you holding signs that say, "I miss you!" or "See you soon!"

If you have friends who live near your partner, try to enlist their help. They can assist you by arranging outings, delivering things on your behalf, or decorating your partner's office to surprise him or her on your anniversary. They simply might keep you informed of what types of things your partner might appreciate. This is especially helpful if you have never lived in the city in which your partner now lives.

The things you can do if money is no object increases exponentially. Rent a billboard in your partner's city, take out a full-page ad in the local newspaper where your partner lives, send a limo to take your partner out for a night on the town — these are just a few things you can do to still "be there" with your partner even when you cannot actually be there. Just because miles separate you, does not mean you cannot be present, even if it is through reminders you send occasionally.

Why bother with these little things? You want to stay connected and make sure your partner knows you are thinking of him or her throughout the day. Being in a long-distance relationship can take quite a bit of effort, and if you fall into a pattern of not acknowledging your partner regularly, the connection between the two of you is going to suffer. Think of your relationship in the same terms as a pet; you can feed your pet and make sure it has water to drink and a place to sleep, but if you never take the time to show the pet affection or to give it treats once in a while, there is a pretty good chance the pet is not going to be happy and content. You relationship might shuffle along and exist, but you want more than mere existence of the relationship — you want a thriving, flourishing relationship. You have to be willing to put forth the effort if you want the relationship to be the best it can be.

Conclusion

The Bright Future Ahead

Being in a successful long-distance relationship can take a lot of work, but it is also something that is absolutely worth all of the effort involved. Every time you feel lonely or frustrated about your situation, try to take a step back and look at the bigger picture. You go through the things you go through, so you eventually can be with the person you are meant to be with. When you think about it, that is a powerful thing. So, although it can be tiring to maintain a long-distance relationship — especially when it is for a long time — it is a time that will help solidify your relationship. If the two of you can manage to flourish together while apart, there is a good chance you can be amazing when together.

Future Dividends

Why do you invest in something today? The answer is simple: You invest today, so you can enjoy dividends tomorrow. The same idea pertains to your long-distance relationship. The effort you put into your relationship today will bring you and your partner closer together and will demonstrate that you are willing to put forth the effort to make things work. Not every relationship gets tested in this way, so when it comes down to it, successfully navigating a long-distance arrangement is a huge advantage. You and your partner know you can stay together even when things get tough and even when you cannot be with each other physically every day. Couples that have never had to maintain their relationships while away from each other might not have the same confidence in knowing that no matter what, they can make it work.

Every time you make an effort to make sure your partner is happy, to making communication more effective, or toward staying out of situations that might harm the bond between you and your partner, you are doing something that will pay off eventually. All of your efforts are like investments; the more you give, the more you are likely to get back, providing you are investing in the right areas.

So, the next time you feel too tired to video chat with your partner, or the next time you get frustrated because the Internet went down during an instant message chat with your partner, take a deep breath, and remember that the frustration you are going through is worth it when you look at the bigger picture. Every time you see a happy couple walking along hand in hand and you feel pangs of jealousy, turn your thoughts toward your partner, and think about how nice it will be when the two of you get the opportunity to walk along hand in hand. Look toward the future with your partner. When you keep the bigger picture in mind, you make decisions based on what is best for your relationship instead of thinking short term and making decisions based on what you want this minute.

Always keep in mind that a flourishing long-distance relationship is far superior to a long-distance relationship in which both of you merely are maintaining the relationship. When a person feels neglected in a relationship, there is a chance that he or she might start to look elsewhere for attention or might stop making an effort to help the relationship get stronger. If you stop putting an effort into your long-distance relationship, your partner might stop putting forth an effort, too. This is not a flourishing relationship — in fact, it is not even a maintained relationship. Instead, it is a doomed relationship.

What changes can you make right now that can make your long-distance relationship even better? Do you have open and frequent communication with your partner? Have the two of you devised a concrete plan for your mutual future? Do you both actively work toward making sure that the other person feels appreciated? If you can answer "yes" to each of these questions, then you are well on your way to a flourishing long-distance relationship. Although it is true that these types of relationships can be stressful and difficult to maintain, it becomes easier to maintain the long-distance arrangement when the relationship is flourishing.

CASE STUDY:
SUCCESS CAN HAPPEN

John, successfully courted his
wife from afar

I met my wife Annie on a dating website designed specifically for Catholic singles. We started out using the website's email and chat service to connect with each other. When we were ready for the next step, we traded email addresses and eventually, gave each other our phone numbers. I had been divorced for ten years and was certainly tired of being alone and lonely, especially because I had lived that entire time out of state from where my family lives. Annie had been divorced and separated for only a few years, but we both knew what it was like to live in an estranged relationship.

Annie always has been a nurturing type, exemplified by her career choice as an LPN (licensed practical nurse). She got my sense of humor from the very beginning and shared some of her favorite "Far Side" comics in one of the earliest cards she sent to me (and I still have them). I was better at texting as far as it came to staying connected, so we regularly exchanged texts, which made it easier for us both to deal with our loneliness. I could not move (due to a custody situation), so I needed to connect with somebody who could move and/or was close. Annie knew this because I had made that very clear in my dating profile on the website. Annie was from the East Coast, but was currently living in Wisconsin, so she was able to visit on long weekends. We traded visits over the next year. After I proposed (in Wisconsin), Annie moved to Michigan to be near enough that we could effectively plan our wedding. The rest, as they say, is history. Annie did an amazing job of sending me notes and cards, and I made sure to keep up on texts and emails as well as phone calls while we were so far apart.

No Problem is Too Big

Nearly every problem the two of you might encounter is something that can be worked through. People who successfully navigate long-distance relationships know this better than most couples because they already have faced physical separation and triumphed in a scenario where many other couples would crumble. When you manage to stay together even when you cannot be physically together, you feel much more able to conquer just about anything.

Make no mistake about it; maintaining a flourishing long-distance relationship is an admirable accomplishment. It is something that you and your partner should be proud of. Consider that for some couples, a physical distance is enough justification to end the relationship. Instead of abandoning the effort and not trying to make it work, you and your partner decided not only to make it work, but also to make it work in a way where you both feel satisfied and appreciated. Love stories are made from this type of stuff.

Be proud of what you and your partner have accomplished, and do not lose sight of the need to keep improving your relationship. If you fall into a rut of merely maintaining the relationship, things might start to fall apart. Actively contribute to your relationship in any way you can, and when problems arise, remind yourself that you and your partner already have leaped over the hurdle of being separated by miles. With this is in mind, it quickly becomes apparent that the two of you can leap over other hurdles, too.

What Does the Future Hold?

Where will the future lead you and your partner? In a best-case scenario, it will lead you to the opportunity to say goodbye to your long-distance arrangement and finally be together for good. When it comes right down to it, a long-distance relationship should be a temporary arrangement for most couples. A few couples can maintain a long-distance relationship on a permanent basis, and those that do so do so by choice instead of out of necessity. For most couples, however, staying in a long-distance relationship forever is not something they are willing to do.

If you and your partner have not made a complete commitment to each other yet, you should at least have plans to see each other face-to-face sometime soon. If, on the other hand, you and your partner are committed to each other completely, then the future should include a definite date for when the relationship will no

longer be long distance. Things should be in motion for the two of you to be together, and you should both agree on how you can both make that happen.

When you think about your future together, you can be sure that by cultivating your relationship and caring about whether your relationship is flourishing, you are giving yourselves a far better chance of lasting than you would have if you just went through the motions of keeping the two of you together. If you and your partner both are willing to work toward the good of your relationship, you will form a strong bond that helps sustain you during tough times. Job loss, illness, and other unexpected problems can sideline relationships that are not already strong; by working toward a solid relationship, you also ready you and your partner to weather the storms that inevitably will come your way.

Appendix

Here you will find a list of some helpful websites including online communication tools, photo sharing, and more. This list is not exhaustive, of course. You can find a huge selection of other resources online by typing "Long Distance Relationship Help" or "LDR Resources" into a search engine.

Tamsen's Tip

Resources online for people in long-distance relationships are staggering. Use the tools available to you, but remember also to turn to friends and family for support. Plenty of people probably are willing to help you if you are willing to ask.

Online Communication

Staying in touch with a long-distance partner has never been easier. Unless your partner is in a radically different time zone or works incredibly long hours, you probably will be able to reach your partner every day to connect.

www.facebook.com: This social networking website allows you to post videos, photos, and status updates. You also can use this website for instant messaging. Facebook is free.

www.gmail.com: Gmail is just one of the many free email services available. A Gmail account also will allow you to blog free through the Google platform, which is another possible option for keeping your partner informed about what is going on in your life. Keep in mind that blogs generally are viewable to everyone.

www.messenger.yahoo.com: Download Yahoo! instant messenger to your computer, or use on your phone. Instant Messaging, photo sharing, and video chat are some of the products offered through Yahoo!

www.skype.com: Use Skype for video calls and voice dialing. Many of the features offered by Skype (including video chat) are free.

www.twitter.com: Post short status updates and photos to stay in touch with your partner using this free website.

Share Photos and Videos

Help your partner feel connected to you by sharing photos and videos. This is fundamentally important if you have children with your partner; sharing photos regularly will help your partner cope how the kids grow while he or she is away. Do not forget to send some print photos through the mail occasionally, too.

www.flickr.com: Upload photos for sharing online on this website. This website is particularly helpful if you want to upload photos to share on more than one social media website.

www.photobucket.com: Another photo sharing website, this website also allows the uploading of videos.

www.youtube.com: Post videos for your partner on this website, but keep in mind they can be seen by others. YouTube® is free.

Games to Share

You do not have to limit your communications with your partner to just chatting. Increase the fun factor in your relationship by indulging in some games that you both enjoy and can play together.

www.chess.com: You and your partner can play chess together using this free website.

www.mmorpg.com: This website offers lists and reviews of the latest MMORPGs (Massive Multiplayer Online Role Playing Game) available. This is a good website to visit if you and your partner want to get involved with online games together, but do not know where to start.

www.pogo.com: This free website offers a wide variety of fun games you can play with your partner in real time.

www.thesims.com: This is the official website for the popular virtual reality game The Sims.

Staying Connected

The options for staying connected are impressive, thanks to the Internet and the wide varieties of companies willing to deliver just about anything anywhere.

www.americangreetings.com: Create e-cards to email to your partner, or purchase paper greeting cards to send through the mail.

www.ftd.com: Use this flower delivery service to order a bouquet of flowers or basket of goodies for your partner.

www.kayak.com: This travel comparison website shows you the least expensive options for travel, which might come in handy when it comes time to visit your partner.

www.timeanddate.com: What time is it where your partner is right now? Use the free tool on this website to figure out.

Help for You

Help is out there, so use some of the free resources available online to make the stress of being apart a little easier to handle.

www.dailystrength.org: An online support group for people in long-distance relationships is just one of the groups offered by this website.

www.lovingfromadistance.com: Here you will find advice and tips on how to make your relationship survive the distance, a supportive community of fellow long distancers, inspiring pages including true LDR stories, as well as other resources relevant to those in "geographically challenged" relationships.

www.militaryspousesupport.net: This website provides valuable resources and tools for military spouses to help them cope with having a spouse deployed.

www.odb.org: The official website for the daily devotional *Our Daily Bread*, you can use this website for daily brief reflective moments.

www.penzu.com: This website provides a free, online journal tool that allows you to journal your feelings. This can be incredibly helpful during times of stress, or when you miss your partner.

Bibliography

Average LDR Statistics. **www.longdistancerelationships.com/advice/article.asp?articleid=9**
Find statistics about long-distance relationships provided by this website dedicated to LDRs.

"Exercise: 7 Benefits of Regular Physical Activity." **www.mayoclinic.com/health/exercise/HQ01676**
Exercise provides myriad benefits, according to the Mayo Clinic.

Landers, Daniel. "The Influence of Exercise on Mental Health." **www.fitness.gov/mentalhealth.htm**
Exercise is not only good for your body but also for your mind as well.

Narayan, Seetha. *The Complete Idiot's Guide to Long-Distance Relationships*. Alpha Books: New York, 2005.
This book is an excellent resource for long-distance couples.

Peterson, Josh. "Green Your Long Distance Relationship: Long distance relationships can work for you and the environment." **http://planetgreen.discovery.com/work-connect/green-long-distance-relationship.html**
Being in a long-distance relationship does not have to be bad for the environment.

Shipp, Sylvia Julann. *The Long Distance Relationship Guidebook: Strengthen Your Relationship from Afar.* 2006.
Shipp offers helpful tips in this book about long-distance relationships.

Tiger, Caroline. *The Long Distance Relationship Guide: Advice for the Geographically Challenged.* Philadelphia: Quirk Books, 2005.
This guide can help you feel connected to your partner while apart.

Author Biography

Tamsen Butler is the author of *The Complete Guide to Personal Finance: For Teenagers and College Students*, which won first place in the Young Adult Non-Fiction category of the 2010 Next Generation Indie Book Awards. In addition to the other books she has written, Tamsen writes for local publications and writes for a variety of websites including LoveToKnow and BabiesOnline. Her two vibrant children (Monet and Abram) keep her on her toes.

Index